UNSEENPRESS.COM'S OFFICIAL

ENCYCLOPEDIA OF

HAUNTED

SOUTHERN

INDIANA

BY
NICOLE KOBROWSKI

Unseenpress.com, Inc. PO Box 687 Westfield, IN 46074

UNSEENPRESS.COM'S OFFICIAL

ENCYCLOPEDIA OF

HAUNTED

SOUTHERN

INDIANA

BY
NICOLE KOBROWSKI

Unseenpress.com, Inc. PO Box 687 Westfield, IN 46074

For information contact:
Unseenpress.com, Inc.
PO Box 687
Westfield, IN 46074

Library of Congress Cataloging-in-Publication Data

Kobrowski, Nicole
    Unseenpress.com's Definitive Encyclopedia of Haunted Indiana/Nicole Kobrowski
            Includes index
  1. Ghosts Indiana; 2. Paranormal Indiana; 3. Indiana History; 4. Indiana Travel

Library of Congress Control Number: 2017900824
ISBN-13: 978-0-9986207-3-2

Printed in the United States of America

Published by
Haunted Backroads Books
an imprint of Unseenpress.com, Inc.
PO Box 687
Westfield, IN 46074

Although the authors and publisher have made every effort to ensure the accuracy and completeness of information contained in this book, we assume no responsibility for errors, inaccuracies, omissions or any inconsistency herein. Any slights of people, places or organizations are unintentional.

The Unseenpress.com, Inc. website is
http://www.unseenpress.com/

Cover design Unseenpress.com, Inc.

NOTES

Table of Contents

OTHER TITLES BY NICOLE KOBROWSKI

Published by Unseenpress.com, Inc.
(print and ebook)

- Haunted Backroads: Central Indiana
- Haunted Backroads: Ghosts of Westfield
- Haunted Backroads: Ghosts of Madison County, Indiana
- Fractured Intentions: A History of Central State Hospital for the Insane
- She Sleeps Well: The Extraordinary Life and Murder of Dr. Helene Elise Hermine Knabe
- Unseenpress.com's Official Encyclopedia of Haunted Indiana
- Unseenpress.com's Official Encyclopedia of Haunted Northern Indiana
- Unseenpress.com's Official Encyclopedia of Haunted Central Indiana
- Unseenpress.com's Official Encyclopedia of Haunted Southern Indiana

Published by IUPUI
Distance Learning: A Guide to System Planning and Implementation

(by Merrill, Young, and Kobrowski)

Published by Bildungsverlag EINS
Metal Line (Instructor's guide and workbook)
Hotel Line (Instructor's Guide)
Englisch für Elektroberufe (Instructor's guide and workbook)
Supply Line (Instructor's guide and workbook)
Construction Line (Instructor's guide and workbook)

Coming soon!
Haunted Backroads: Ghosts of Hamilton County, Indiana
Audio books

Dedication

Spring showers
Summer breezes
Fall leaves
and
Winter winds

These are the things Indiana is made of.

Sometimes all on the same day.

About the Author

Nicole Kobrowski is the co-owner of Unseenpress.com, Inc., which was founded in 2001. She and her husband Michael started the business because of their interest in the paranormal and their love of history. She has written professionally under a variety of pen names for over 20 years, including books for ESL and dozens of articles on a myriad topics. Being a paranormal enthusiast for over 30 years, she has done investigation work in many areas including spirit photography, electronic voice phenomenon, and automatic writing. In addition to her work in the paranormal field, Nicole is an Adult Education Consultant. Currently, she lives in her "über haunted home" with her husband and Lyla, their rescued cat.

Preface

Every book I write is a creative pleasure. With this particular book, I need to learn to cut the cord. Every time I was about to finish and send it off, someone (sometimes me) would let me know about another fascinating place that I think just has to be included.

When I originally wrote the book, I had been to about 33% of these locations. As of this writing, I have been to over 70%. By the next writing, I will have completed my goal of visiting every site listed.

As always, the intent of this book is to educate and to serve as a guide for paranormal enthusiasts, investigators and anyone traveling around the wonderful state of Indiana.

Special thanks to Emily Dickos-Carter and to Megan Norris.

I hope you enjoy it as much as I enjoyed writing it.

Nicole Kobrowski
January 2017

We love hearing from paranormal enthusiasts and investigators about their experiences at these locations or from other "haunted' locations. Send all enquiries or story submissions for future publications to customerservice@ unseenpress.com.

A Guide to the Encyclopedia

This book is set up in order for you to find information quickly and easily. The book is set up by counties, which you'll find at the top of each page. For each entry, I've developed a legend for your use as follows:

Sample Entry

Old St. Louis Cemetery	The name of the location.
Hope: South of 800 N on 670 E	The directions, address and supporting information.
Visitors captured orbs on film and video. One investigator left hurriedly after he saw a group of transparent people carrying a wooden coffin .	The section entry contains background on events around the history and haunting.

Do-It-Yourself Investigations

Since starting Unseenpress.com, Inc. we've been approached by people and organizations on a weekly basis asking us if we'd investigate their home or asking if they can go with us to a "ghost hunt" or an "investigation". These aren't even including the places we approach for investigations. Unfortunately, we can't accommodate all requests- days only have 24 hours. As a result, we've referred some people to reputable paranormal groups so they connect with investigators in their area and we've worked with clients to find them reputable help in their area. Also, we have taken some experienced investigators on our investigations and had great success with it. We have also started education classes for people who want to take responsibility for their own hauntings. We'll talk more about that later.

Still, we find a fundamental difference in some of the requests- "ghost hunt" and "investigation". Both terms have very different meanings. Certain people want to go to haunted locations, be scared, talk about what they've experienced, make a quick determination it is haunted (or not) and move on to the next location. Other people want to conduct investigations that are scientifically documented, following set procedures.

Before you go
Your team should have a clear idea of who they are and how they should behave before they ever set foot on the client's property. Standards should be explained and reviewed before the investigation.

Before you decide to go, we recommend the following standards:

- Get permission (See Permission section).
- Walk the area before the investigation. If you're doing a daytime investigation, this is not so important. If you're doing a night time investigation, you should do this step to understand where you might encounter difficulty. You should always do a walk through to understand the temperature fluctuations and EMF readings (however, how will you really know what a baseline is? You could be experiencing paranormal activity on your first visit).
- Meet at the location and decide who will do what and with what equipment.
- Offer a blessing, protection, or prayer if you wish.
- Walk around to decide where to place equipment.
- Take pictures, videos and audio recordings. Make notes about any changes in temperature, feelings you had or sightings. If everyone on your team does this, you should have an accurate picture of the investigation when you're finished. It helps eliminate non-paranormal causes for suspected activity.

Once you've made the necessary arrangements, consider the following points during an investigation.

- Never roam alone in an unfamiliar setting. You need to be safe.
- Take ID with you. You might need to prove who you are.
- Take a cell phone with you and let others know where you are going.
- If you will be in the field for a long time, take adequate food and drink with you. Eat only in specific areas to minimize noise and contamination of evidence.
- If you are asked to leave, do so without making a fuss. It will benefit you in the long run. Respect everyone

living and dead.
- Don't smoke. It can contaminate photographic/video evidence.
- Use care when taking photos. Don't take photos when others are taking them. Note anything that could create false orbs in photos. Keep hair, fingers and camera straps away from the lens. You, equipment, or other items can cast false positive shadows so be aware of your location and equipment placement.
- Do not move audio recorders when speaking. It can create distortion.
- No drugs or alcohol before, during or after an investigation. If you're sick, stay home. Illegal drugs are a no. Drunk people on an investigation or after an investigation while still a part of the team is stupid and not good for the paranormal field or its image.
- Record any conditions that could affect data (humidity, dust, etc.).
- No noisy clothing, jewelry, keys, or change- these items affect what we hear.
- Apply no items that affect smell- cologne, perfume, etc. Do use fragrance-free deodorant.
- Dress for the field. Use your team's uniform or wear clean, weather appropriate clothes.
- Ensure hair is away from face- ponytails are good. Buns are even better.
- If you are frightened in a location- leave. Some of the most haunted places are in the middle of nowhere and you might have a bad encounter with a human. Use common sense.
- Have an emergency plan and make sure someone is on the team that is able to perform CPR and/or call for help quickly.

Paranormal Investigation

The Field
Much information is written about paranormal investigation. Some of it is stated in absolute terms. Paranormal investigation is a wide open field. I say field, because that is what it should be, however, to my knowledge, no one makes a living solely by investigating the paranormal- myself included. Certainly, research labs exist for parapsychology, which is completely different than paranormal investigation. Most investigators belong to organizations that support paranormal research, though, most everyone has a day job.

Education Options
Along these same lines, there are no accredited degrees in paranormal investigation. None. Zero. Nada. Niet, Kein. Don't even waste your time and money. Many paranormal organizations offer certificate courses to become "certified" in paranormal investigation. Many paranormal groups charge dues and ask you to take classes (sometimes paying extra) in order to be "qualified" to go on investigations. As a lifelong student of Adult Education, I can hardly argue about basic training needed to safely go on an investigation. However, each organization has its own policies and procedures for accomplishing an investigation. You have to decide if they are sound, if you agree with them and if you'd like to be a part of the organization.

Knowing the state of education in the paranormal field, this difference begs the question, "what does being a certified paranormal investigator (or obtaining a certificate) get me? Some people believe it doesn't really benefit you. As it isn't a recognized field of work or science (yes, we are considered pseudo-scientists), it isn't going to raise your pay (unless you latch onto the media). Some people would argue the benefit comes in being certified to investigate with the organization that certified you. Other people argue that being certified or recognized by a certain group is motivation enough. They believe that this certification might get them into more places or give them more of an advantage. Again, it is up to your interpretation.

Media, Myths and Absolutes

No one, no matter what experiences someone has had with the paranormal, knows what to expect or what concrete facts can be said about spirit activity. No one can concretely define what a ghost really is or if they exist. While I have definitions of some of the elements surrounding the paranormal and investigation, my take may be different than another investigator's definition. Also, I have most definite feelings about ghosts; I am a firm believer in them. Some people are out to disprove the existence of spirits.

The media also has its own take on the paranormal ranging from the cheesy "ghostbusters" type attitude to making it somewhat darker and more dramatic than what it really is. For example, shows exist for ratings. If television shows didn't have something scary and exciting, no one would watch them. Be careful what you consume.

Also, be careful about what you read and absorb. For example, an investigator on a popular television series said "A human spirit can only lift three to ten pounds." Really? How do we know this? Did this investigator have an interview with a ghost? Because if he did, I would love the transcript. Does this mean that when Arnold Schwarzenegger dies he is limited to lifting three to ten pounds? Or does he get to lift more because he was a body builder? Likewise another misconception is that the "haunting hours" are between 12-3am. If that were true, why do we have so many daytime reports of activity?

Absolute statements like the ones above are patently false until proven otherwise. If someone says conclusively, "Yep, you've got ghosts.", it is their own flavor and opinion- kind of like a certification that your house is haunted. Other investigators may disagree with the findings. While some people believe that ghosts can go home with you (as I do), there are other investigators who do not believe this.

If we can't prove anything what is the point?

All we can do is conduct inquiry based on common assumptions and draw our own conclusions. However, surrounding investigative inquiry is more than just our opinions and biases. We also must take scientific method into account. In scientific inquiry, we decide what we're going to study, decide on an explanation for what we're studying, define how we'll research it, muse on the types of results you think you'll get, execute and analyze the plan. Scientific method is scientific method, no matter what area you are in. I am a scholar in Adult Education and I apply scientific method the same as anyone who has learned it. The focus of my research in Adult Education is different than that of a Sociologist.

You might ask what the problem is, that scientific inquiry seems very straightforward. It is, but what is contained in each step is the difference between mainstream, accepted science and the assumed pseudo-science of the paranormal. We can't test against what we don't know. Our tools have only been test driven to a certain point. For example, many investigators believe EMF detectors can indicate spirit activity. How do we know they aren't picking up power inside the walls, under the floor, etc.? There is a scale for what is normal for certain types of electromagnetic fields, but have we been able to consistently replicate what we're seeing as "abnormal" to be able to say it is truly abnormal and paranormal?

Organizations and Investigations

Investigators employ several steps involved in paranormal investigation. Investigations aren't always exciting and many of them are hurry up and wait situations. Sometimes you get a hit and sometimes after hours of sitting or hours of analyzing, you get nothing. It can be frustrating, but also rewarding. The difference amoung investigators is how they conduct themselves, their groups and their investigations.

One bad experience can lead to a complete distaste for the paranormal in general. Two recent cases come to mind. First, the producers of a show about ghost children did an unauthorized ghost hunt and filiming in Crown Hill Cemetery in Indianapolis, Indiana. While I believe there is much paranormal activity afoot in the cemetery, the cemetery staff made it quite clear that it wants nothing to do with the paranormal. The makers of the program misrepresented the history of the subject and also the history of Crown Hill. Additionally, they didn't ask permission to film on the grounds. They seemed to assume that because it was a cemetery, owned by the State (not true), it was fair game (also not true).

Another example is Central State Hospital also in Indianapolis. A "documentary" was produced on the premise that it would be historic in nature. It was historic all right, but not the historic documentary that was presented in the proposal to the city. Would you want to be affiliated with an organization that misrepresents itself?

Reputation

Moving to the practical, keep in mind that the reputation of your organizations, investigations, and personal behavior is under scrutiny from the minute you approach an organization or individual about conducting an investigation. How you conduct your organization, investigations and/or personal behavior determine how much credibility each element has and how the paranormal community is perceived as a whole. For example, a group of investigators trespassed on a site where a well known serial killer lived. They took pictures and video and posted both on their website and a video sharing site. They even boasted about it on television. When the owner saw this evidence, the police became involved. What do you think about this group's ethics or credibility? I certainly wouldn't want to work with this group. Another group trespassed at Central State Hospital, several times. They were told by the police to stay away from the site but didn't. Now, they have a bad reputation with the police and have given paranormal investigation a bad name. Would you want these people coming into your home or business?

Permission

Investigation doesn't mean glory. Too many times have I seen investigators jockey for position while investigating hauntings. With the exception of private homes, businesses, etc. any already known location has been investigated or hunted to some extent many time over. There is no "scooping" going on. For example, Central State Hospital in Indianapolis is the perceived as the Holy Grail of haunted locations. Who hasn't been out there? Most folks who have been here are employees, with the police or have done so illegally. What does claiming "first rights" do? Absolutely nothing. What does the trespassing do to the credibility of you, your organization and to the field? *Trespassing kills credibility.*

Many people say, "well how do you get in there?" or "I don't know how to get permission." Well, here's your guide. Find the owner and get permission. *Always get it in writing.*

Find the Owner
Property, including businesses, historic properties, "abandoned" properties, farms, woods, etc.

Go to the township or county recorder and ask for the name of the owner on record for the property. This is public information that they have to give you. You can usually get a phone number as well. Contact the owners and if they don't respond, follow up. If they still don't respond or you get a resounding, "No," let it go. Remember, what you do and how you act reflects on not just you and your organization, but on everyone. Think about how you can revisit it at a future time and maybe change the no to a yes.

Cemeteries
Go to the township trustee, who usually controls them. If your county has a cemetery commission, speak with them. If it is a large cemetery like Crown Hill that is run by an organization, talk to them. If it is a cemetery attached to a church, talk to the pastor, minister, priest, etc. Don't assume that because it is a cemetery that you can visit it any time you wish. Most cemeteries in Indiana close at dusk. Simply calling the police to let them know you're out there doesn't cover you. It is still under the control of others.

Roads and Highways
For your own safety, if nothing else, you must have permission to create an obstruction or to be on these roads. If you are walking on the road, you run the risk of getting yourself killed. If you're with several people, you increase your risk. Many of the haunted roads are in areas where people live.

Once an organized ghost hunting group decided to trespass on a fairly well known area in Hamilton County. They even posted pictures on the internet showing them trespassing. The police were alerted by the owner and they received a notice telling them to take down all photos, videos, etc and that next time they would be prosecuted. How would you like to ask the boss at your day job for bail money?

County Map

The map on the following page shows a numbered county map. On the next page, these numbers correspond with the correct county.

Use the names as a quick reference to find the correct county in the book.

COUNTY MAP OF INDIANA

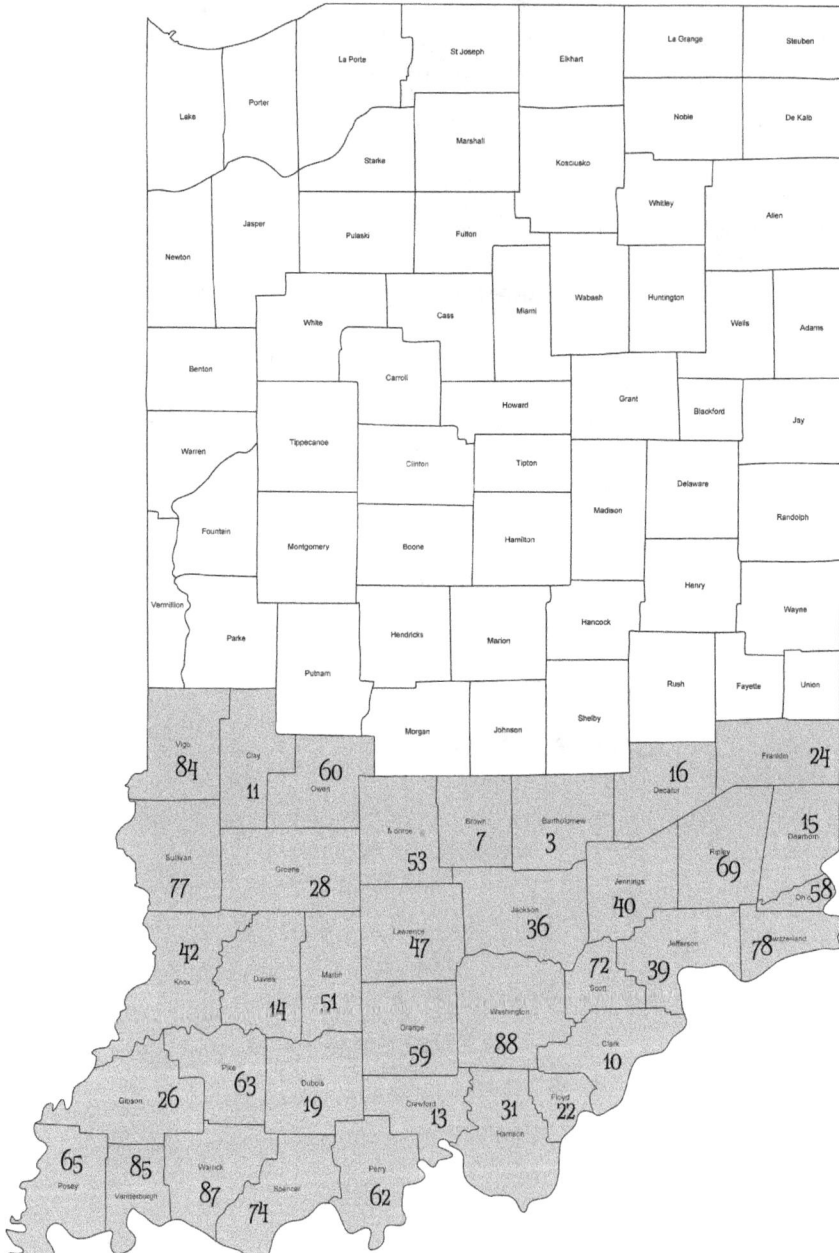

La Porte · St Joseph · Elkhart · La Grange · Steuben
Lake · Porter · Noble · De Kalb
Starke · Marshall · Kosciusko
Jasper · Whitley · Allen
Newton · Pulaski · Fulton
White · Cass · Miami · Wabash · Huntington · Wells · Adams
Benton · Carroll · Howard · Grant · Blackford · Jay
Warren · Tippecanoe · Clinton · Tipton · Delaware · Randolph
Fountain · Montgomery · Boone · Hamilton · Madison
Vermillion · Henry · Wayne
Parke · Hendricks · Marion · Hancock
Putnam · Rush · Fayette · Union
Morgan · Johnson · Shelby

84 Vigo · Clay · 60 Owen · 16 Decatur · Franklin 24
11
77 Sullivan · Greene · 53 Monroe · 7 Brown · 3 Bartholomew · 69 Ripley · 15 Dearborn
28 · Jennings 40 · 58 Ohio
42 Knox · Lawrence 47 · Jackson 36 · Jefferson · 78 Switzerland
14 Daviess · 51 Martin · 72 Scott · 39
59 Orange · 88 Washington · 10 Clark
26 Gibson · 63 Pike · 19 Dubois · 13 Crawford · 31 Harrison · 22 Floyd
65 Posey · 85 Vanderburgh · Warrick · Spencer · Perry
87 · 74 · 62

ALPHABETICAL LIST OF INDIANA COUNTIES

Number	Name	Number	Name
3	Bartholomew	60	Owen
7	Brown	62	Perry
10	Clark	63	Pike
11	Clay	65	Posey
13	Crawford	69	Ripley
14	Daviess	72	Scott
15	Dearborn	74	Spencer
16	Decatur	77	Sullivan
19	Dubois	78	Switzerland
22	Floyd	82	Vanderburgh
24	Franklin	84	Vigo
26	Gibson	87	Warrick
28	Greene	88	Washington
31	Harrison		
36	Jackson		
39	Jefferson		
40	Jennings		
42	Knox		
47	Lawrence		
51	Martin		
53	Monroe		
58	Ohio		
59	Orange		

BARTHOLOMEW
COUNTY

1130 25th Street
Columbus: 1130 25th St.
(aka Subway Restaurant on 46)

Shadow figures walk through the store. Patrons and employees hear voices when no one else is around.

Ceraland Recreation Area
Columbus: Off 525 E. south of SR 46 and north of SR 7.

In the 1970s, a woman drowned while crossing the creek during a flood. You can see and hear her crying on the edge of the banks.

Crump Theatre
Columbus: 425 3rd St.
(aka The Crump, Crump Opera Hall and Theatre)

According to Rovene Quigley, executive director of the Crump Theatre, she is never alone in the 1800s building. Many stories exist about this historic theater, including Quigley finding an extra $86.50 in her receipt box, and a helpful ghost finding a boiler inspection certificate and placing it on her desk.

Visitors see orbs, mists and apparitions in this theater. Temperature drops and spikes occur preceding these events. EVPs caught in the building include male and female's voices. Some topics of conversation include "That was fun.", "What was that", "I wish they'd leave.", and "What are they doing?"

Elizabethtown
Elizabethtown: Elizabethtown is located between US 31 and SR 7 on CR E475S (Legal Tender Rd./2nd St.)

At the edge of town by the welcome sign a woman in black will stare at you as you drive into town.

Hartsville College Cemetery
Hartsville: South end of East St.

This is the original site of the coeducational United Brethren school. It was founded 1850 as Hartsville Academy by a public act of the Indiana General Assembly. The campus moved four blocks south, circa 1865 and was destroyed by fire in January 1898. Many graduates became distinguished citizens in their communities throughout the state and nation.

Several serious looking young men walk through the cemetery in the day and night. One young man chases a woman in a hoop skirt into the woods on the south east side of the cemetery.

Haunted House
Columbus: House at west corner of SR 11 and CR W200S.

Visitors hear noises. Metallic clangs heard throughout home, especially on first floor. Whispers from male and female voices are also heard.

Haw Creek Baptist Cemetery
Hope: CR S200E at E. Stafford Rd.

Shadow people dart between headstones. One investigator was chased by a shadow figure through the cemetery and back to a nearby church. A vortex and white apparitions have also surprised visitors.

North High School
Columbus: 1400 25th St.

A child named "Mikey" was run down by a buggy on a road that used to be where the school is now. The auditorium is believed to be exactly where he was killed. Mikey runs on the stage, in the sound booth and up on the catwalk. He also turns lights on and off.

Old St. Louis Cemetery
Hope: South of 800 N on 670 E

Visitors captured orbs on film and video. One investigator left hurriedly after he saw a group of transparent people carrying a wooden coffin .

Petersville House
Petersville: Unknown. Rumored to have burned.

Orbs and a bright white female figure were seen at this location. The exact location of this house is unknown, but it is suggested that it was located anywhere from downtown Petersville to any number of empty country lots.

Quality Machine and Tool
Columbus: 1201 Michigan Ave.

An employee hung himself over a failed relationship with a woman. Employees and customers have seen his shadowy figure as well as other spirits. Employees find that things go missing, but are returned to odd places.

Roberts Cemetery
Edinburgh: CR W1200S east of CR S500W (east of Edinburgh) Bartholomew County/ Shelby County line.

Investigators captured orbs on film. An EVP of a woman asking where her husband has been heard.

Seventeenth Street Railroad Bridge
Columbus: Go into the park at the end of 17th St. Walk the path leading into the woods. You will see a tunnel that goes under the tracks with a steep gravel incline. Climb to the top of the tracks and the bridge will be to your right.

A woman in the 1920s had an illegitimate child and was driven to throw herself and her child off the bridge. They found her body but not the baby's body. A creature with two legs and yellow eyes haunts the bridge. Sometiems the cries of a baby can be heard. During a full moon the mother of the baby appears and she calls out to her baby. People report footsteps following them through the area.

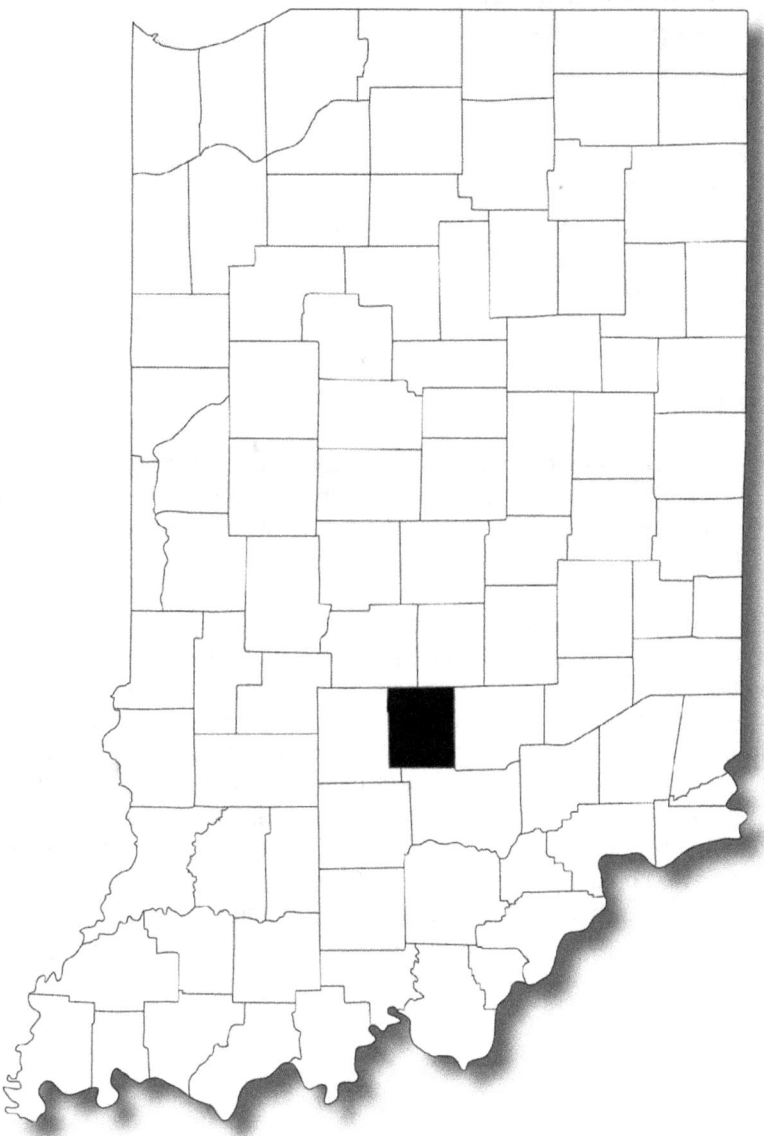

BROWN COUNTY

Podunk (aka Brown County State Park)

Nashville: Brown Co. State Park off Bond Cemetery Rd.
(See also Bargersville, Johnson Co.)
(aka Brown County State Park)

A baby crawls on the road and sometimes it laughs and cries. Emotional outbursts, physical touches (pushing and scratching) plague visitors. One version of the stories at this location includes a phantom truck that will follow you. Many people have reportedly seen this truck and lights that appear and disappear just as quickly. Visitors have taken photos of strange mists and half apparitions. One investigator claims to have taken a picture of a satyr.

Story Inn

Nashville: 6404 S. SR 135

The Story Inn used to be a general store in what was once Storyville. Dr. George Story established the small town in 1851. The original structure burned down in 1915 and was rebuilt. Today, Story Inn is a restaurant, as well as four bed and breakfast units. It is also comprised of ten other little cottages.

Several paranormal events occur regularly at this location and many ghost hunters spend the night at the inn. In the Blue Lady room, one can summon the spirit by turning on a blue light next to the bed. She primps at the dresser. She interacts with guests, and has clawed one man in the shower. The Blue Lady also whispers to guests and hypnotizes them with her lovely blue eyes. Other occurrences include objecgts moving such as coffee pots and candles. Pictures slide off walls, tables, and shelves. Smells of baby powder and cherry tobacco fill the air. Visitors hear chatting and footsteps upstairs when no one is around. Guests experience severe temperature drops. Wine was thrown in the owner's face. A spectral man in brown has been seen in the kitchen. People are regularly pinched and poked. The staff hears whispers throughout the inn. Visitors and investigators report orbs and a picture captured a transparent woman looking out a window.

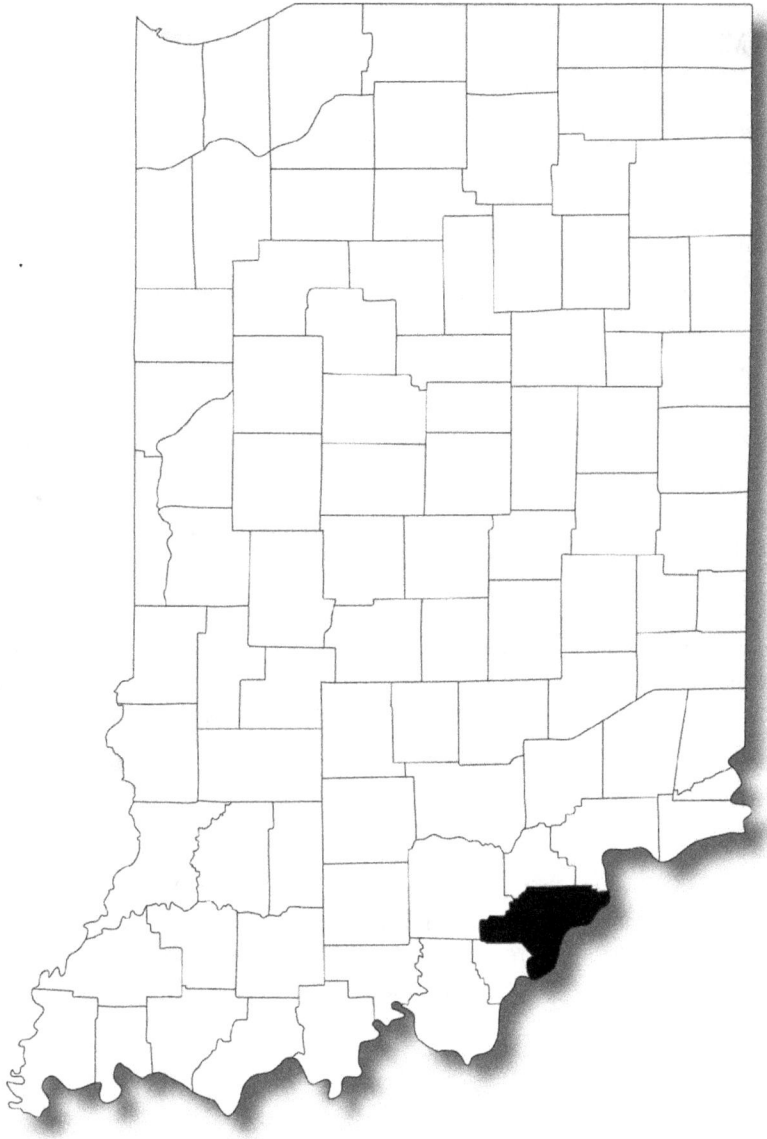

CLARK
COUNTY

10 Penny Bridge

Charlestown: Tunnel Mill Rd.
(aka Tunnel Mill Road Bridge)

A man died on the bridge. As the story goes if you put 10 pennies on the bridge in a straight line (not stacked) the pennies will scatter over the bridge or disappear.

Blackston Mill Road

Utica: Blackston Mill Rd. (where road dips)
(aka Deadman's Hollow)

This road was the site where illegal slaves were hanged. It is called Deadman's Hollow because a man was found dead in the area. Investigators hear the scrape of rope on trees, hear unearthly moans and see several men hanging in the trees. When they saw these apparitions, it was as if they were in a time warp and they could see the crowd of people watching them hang.

Brick Church Road Cemetery

Sellersburg: Brick Church Rd. east of Tom Combs Rd.

This cemetery has a glowing green tombstone. Depending on the source of your story, the tombstone that glows changes throughout the cemetery. Some investigators have reported seeing transparent cloaked figures in the church and cemetery during the day and night.

Census Bureau Warehouses

Jeffersonville: 1201 E 10th St.

These buildings are full of paranormal activity. Boxes of heavy paper fall as if feather-light. Radios turn on and lights turn off and on at will. Local history indicates that the area was a holding camp for Germans during WWII and investigators have captured EVPs of men speaking German. Security guards sometimes refuse to go into buildings. (B66 was the infirmary and supposedly the most haunted.)

Charlestown High School

Charlestown: 1 Pirate Place

A girl fell from the catwalk and now haunts the auditorium. She turns lights off and on and walks though the auditorium. You can hear her footsteps on the floor and on the catwalk.

Colgate Palmolive Factory
Clarksville: 1410 S. Clark Blvd.

This factory used to be Indiana State Prison South. Prisoners were mistreated and the female inmates were prostituted to guards and prisoners. The basement is haunted by these prisoners. Apparitions of women chase you through the basement. Some male and female investigators have been scratched by unseen hands.

Dan's Run
Henryville: Corner of Pixley Knob Rd. and Mountain Grove Rd.

Daniel Guthrie was murdered and buried near Pixley Knob Road and Cemetery Hill (see Mountain Grove Cemetery entry). For over a year, the body remained there until it was found and reburied in Mt. Zion Cemetery. The original burial hole is about four feet deep and still can be seen near the edge of the woods.

People who live in the area see a young man with a handlebar moustache. Additionally, people in the area hear footsteps and experience other paranormal activity, including finding footprints outside windows, muddy shoe prints appearing inside the house, objects levitating and male voices whispering. Some investigators believe the negative energy from Dan's unsolved murder has created a portal for paranormal activity.

Investigators have captured EVPs with a male voice crying out for help and screaming until his voice fades away. Another similar EVP reveals a scream that is accentuated with what sounds like a knife being "pulled in and out of a pumpkin". Visitors to the creek have heard disembodied voices, and have seen mysterious shadows crossing the road in front of headlights at night, although no one is seen. One person ran away from the creek because she heard growling nearby. This unseen growling beast followed closely behind until the woman heard it give a "mournful cry" and then it was silent.

Haymaker House
Charlestown: 14 E. Market St.

Built by Isaac Haymaker around 1870, this home belonged to the family for many years. Close knit as this community is, the families stayed around Charlestown. Many are buried in the local cemetery. can be found in the local cemetery. Several family members had their funerals conducted in the home.

The sound of glass, such as a bottle, falling and rolling, is heard. Pets avoid the upstairs. Banging has been heard in the dining room. Lights turn mysteriously on and off, and light fixtures sway in an absent breeze. Temperatures change from hot to cold. Residents hear their names called although no one is around. The front porch swing sways with invisible visitors while no wind is felt. Items fall from shelves and out of locked cabinets. Phantom figures move around the back yard. Voices are heard in the kitchen. Moans as if someone is in pain are heard. Shades in the home all rolled up at the same time; another time, they went up, down, up, as if someone was pulling them manually. A former owner heard the phone ring and heard strange music playing on the answering machine. Even after she turned it off and unplugged it, the music continued.

Howard Steamboat Museum
Clarksville : 1101 E Market St.

James Howard stands in the basement wearing a top hat.

Jeffersonville High School
Jeffersonville: 2315 Allison Ln.

A woman roams the auditorium. She sits in a corner and when she is spoken to, she stares at you and disappears. Additionally, items in the auditorium move and people have been pushed and have fallen. At one time a construction worker was killed by falling off a ladder- some people believe he was pushed. He's been seen on a ladder on the right side of the auditorium.

Mountain Grove Cemetery
(aka Cemetery Hill)
Henryville: Corner of Pixley Knob Rd. and Mountain Grove Rd.

(See Dan's Run entry, Henryville, Clark Co.)

Investigators hear voices hissing incoherent words. Visitors speculate that this manifestation could be in connection with some of the activity from Dan's Run.

Mount Zion Cemetery
Henryville: At the east end of Henryville Bluelick Rd. and Mt. Zion Rd.

A green hazy lady walks through Mt. Zion Cemetery, sometimes jumping on cars and leaving a sticky residue. She is said to be a woman who was killed on Blue Lick Road after a car accident.

Old Man Ike's
Sellersburg: Stricker Road across from a meat processing facility; near the old Essroc Cement Corp.

Supposedly a man named Ike killed family members in the house. Ike worked at the meat facility and came home one day and chopped his family with a cleaver. Screams are heard at all hours of the day and night.

St. Joe Road Cemetery
Sellersburg: SR 111 east on St. Joe Rd.

There is a hanging tree in the middle of the cemetery. At night, you can see one, or several men hanging from it.

Sunset Grill Restaurant
Clarksville: 318 W. Lewis and Clark Pkwy.
(aka Strattos)

This restaurant was formerly the McCullough Steak House, but was a family home. Originally, guests and employees have heard weird noises in the building. Some mornings employees will come in the restaurant, and all the light bulbs will be unscrewed and sitting on the tables.

Theatre X
Utica : 4505 US 31 East
(Note: Theatre X is an adult entertainment venue.)

A mysterious, transparent man in old work clothes shuffles through the theater. Several of the patrons have also seen a pale woman with blond hair walk near the booths and disappear before their eyes.

Witches Castle
Utica: Upper River Rd. near Quarry Bluff
(aka Mistletoe Falls)

Allegedly witches lived in the house and a group of townspeople ran them out. A transparent apparition of a 7-8 year old girl has been seen and her laugh is heard in the woods. She is also seen as a mist in the home. She has long black hair that covers her face. Several sources claim this area is where Shanda Sharer died but this is untrue.

In a small shack behind the home: Male and female voices are heard. Many apparitions are seen peering out. Two investigators saw apparitions in the shack and its door opened. Two apparitions came out and started walking toward the investigators. Both of them (whether nerves or fact) felt that is was a malevolent force coming toward them and they ran away.

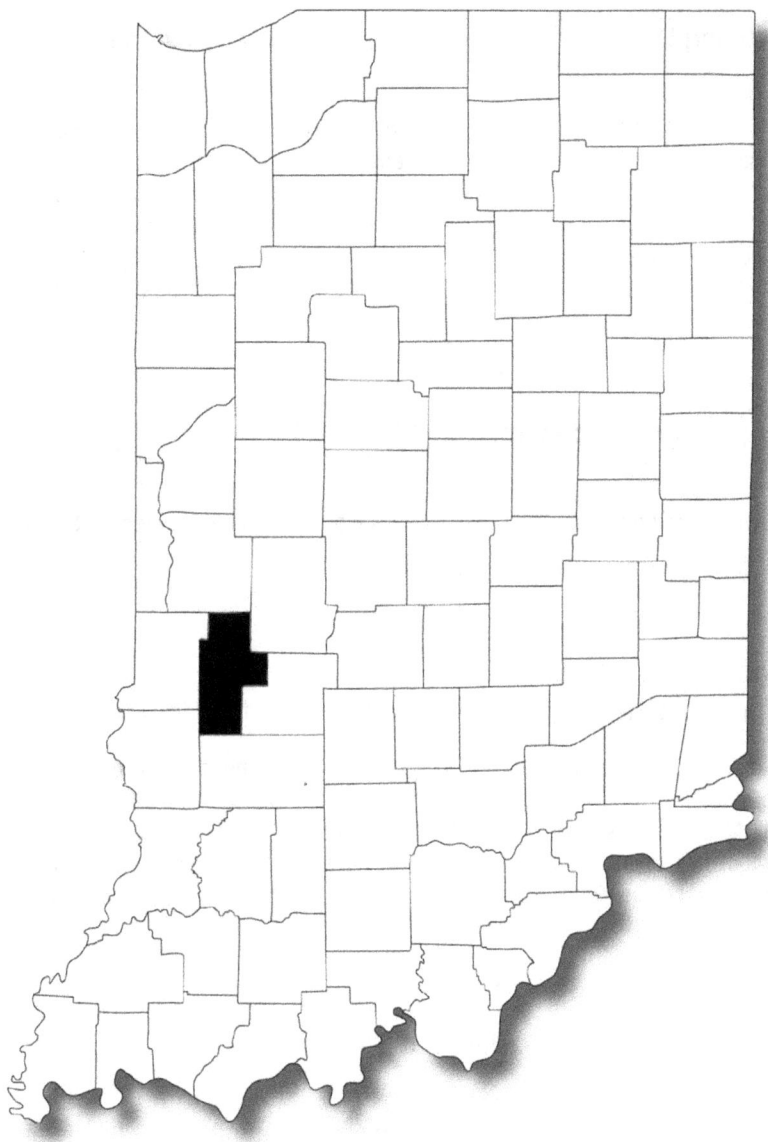

CLAY
COUNTY

Carpenters Cemetery

Brazil: West of SR340 and US40 on CR675. Located next to a jog in the road.
(aka 100 Steps Cemetery)

This cemetery dates back to the late 1860s. At night, count the steps as you ascend to the top of the cemetery. When you've reached 100 the old caretaker will float by you in a semi-transparent state. Some versions of this story say he will predict the future for you. He tells you to leave. If you count the same amount of stairs going back down, your future is supposed to be good. Otherwise, you might be joining the caretaker on the other side! If you avoid the steps, an unknown force pushes people and leaves handprints (or other marks) on them. During the day, you won't count 100 steps. However, visitors witness the figure of a slender woman in a white gown during the day.Strange, misty shapes appear on film.

Haunted Church

Brazil: 300W, in the opposite direction from Spooklight Hill
(See Spooklight Hill, Brazil, Clay Co.)

Lights and mysterious phantoms roam the church. Additionally, visitors feel chilling breezes when the trees are perfectly still.

Hell's Gate

Brazil: Take IN 59 north to CR1350. Continue on this road until you reach Rock Run Rd. Follow Rock Run Rd. until it turns. At the turn you should see the Hell's Gate.

For years, this old railroad underpass has been the source of legends for years. The most common one claims that a train crashed at the location killing, everyone. If you go through the tunnel and wait 10 minutes, a supposed method of death is scribbled on the wall. Mists and orbs collect in pictures. Numerous psychics, the curious, and investigators visit the spot in hopes of finding proof of paranormal activity. Some psychic have violent feelings towards themselves and the area in general. Other people hear screams, laughing, and loud crashes. EVPs of children crying and women speaking have been recorded.

Masonic Lodge

Brazil: Southwest corner of Sherfey and Jackson Streets
(aka Blue Lodge of Masons)

A singing ghost haunts the one time Masonic Lodge. Originally called "the Blue Lodge of Masons", visitors have been pulled, pushed, and touched a variety of times in a variety of places.

The Plantation

Brazil: From the SR 59 and SR 42 intersection, take SR 42 East about 7 miles until you come across Boy Scout Road. Turn north on this road and go about 1.2 miles and you will come to a lane on your right side.

The old shed to the left of the lane leads you back to the ruins of an old home and out buildings. At one time the barns had lofts that were said to be home to the ghosts of the people who used to live at the home. Largely friendly in nature, these ghosts would be doing work in the barn. If they saw you, they would smile, stare and then return to their work.

Poland Chapel

Poland: E. Ohio and Cherry Sts.
(aka Poland Cemetery)

A five year old boy buried here was taken over by "demons"- or at least he began speaking in tongues and acting age-inappropriately. His picture on his gravestone is said to have horns. investigators who believe the child was possessed by demons think the physical manifestation occurred both inside and outside the child. Pictures taken at the cemetery do seem to have some anomalies, including the outline of horns, on his headstone, and the faces of the investigators are blurred. The woods to the rear of the cemetery are home to several transparent figures. including children, men and women. They do not interact, but walk slowly through the trees at night.

Spook Light Hill

Brazil: Take IN 59 north out of Brazil. About 5 miles out you will come to a gravel road that takes you to Carbon. Turn right. On this road, there are three hills. Go to the third and look back at the second. Some people believe any of these hills is Spooklight Hill.

Because this is legend, many people can't agree which of the three hills is the real Spook Light Hill. As the story goes, a ghostly father is looking for his daughter's head. She was decapitated in a car accident or a buggy accident. He appears in the form of a light coming down the road or in the woods. Others have seen him as a shadow figure walking to the left or right of the hill. For a couple of visitors, the man has been known to ask if you've seen her head. On occasion, the girl herself makes an appearance as a headless apparition to the west.

Zion Gummere Cemetery

Brazil: Zion Church Rd. between CR525 and CR100.
(aka Zion Church Cemetery)

A spectre appears and tells you to go back the way you came. Local people believe this is a bad omen. Investigators believe this is someone trying to warn you about something that has happened in the past. Unexplained lights, sensing presences, and hearing whispers are also a part of the paranormal activity here.

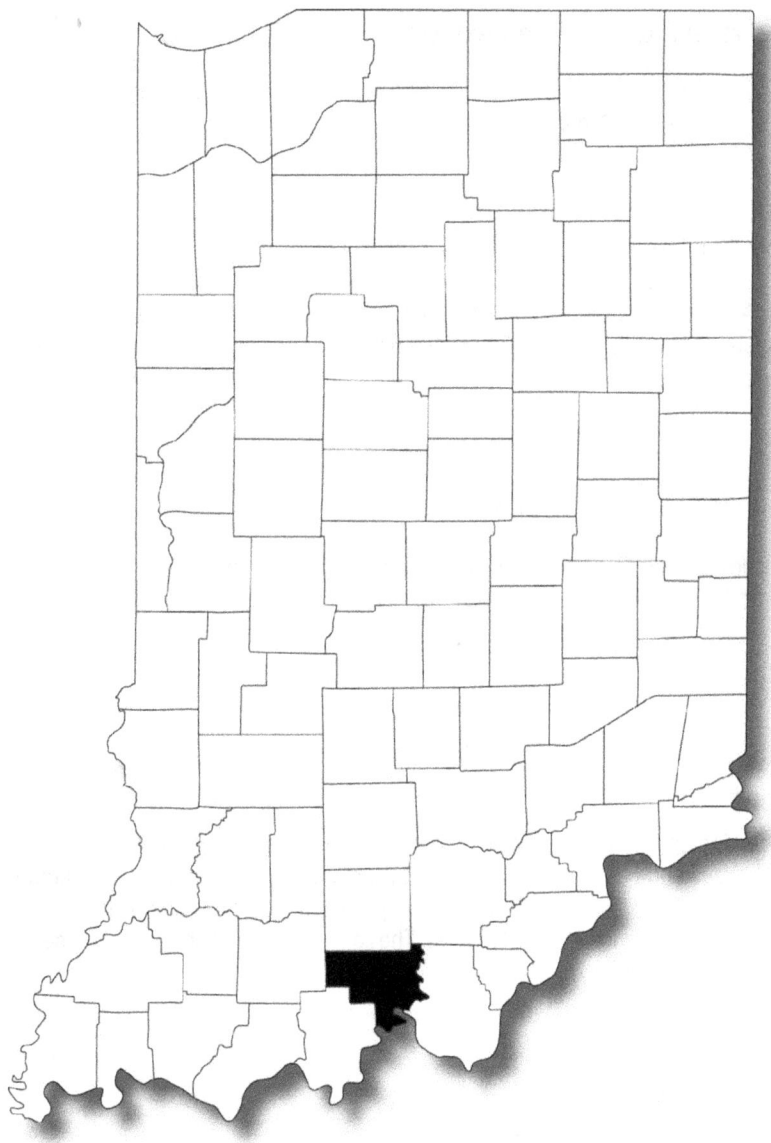

CRAWFORD COUNTY

Carl Smith House
Marengo: Burned and razed. Used to be next to the post office.

Former owners report lights off and on. The house is rumored to be a portal. These events are attributed to many people dying in the home and area surrounding it, it burned and was razed.

Devil's Washboard
Milltown: E Rothrocks Mill Rd. east of Burgess Circle Rd. NW

Considered magical by New Age believers, people come from far and wide to capture a little of the water that flows through this area and give praise for the area. Because of these activities. Visitors report many shadows, fairies and other occurrences, due to these activities.

Marengo Caves
Marengo: IN 64 to SR 64 (400 East SR 64)

Two children, Orris and Blanche Heistand, found the cave in 1883. Public tours began that year. Men with pickaxes and work clothes have been seen in the cave. Investigators believe them to be diamond hunters who were killed shortly after the cave opened.

Old English
Old English: US 64 SW of N. Brownstown Rd.
(precursor to English, Indiana)

The Federal government moved Old English because it was in a flood plain. During the move, the old town was abandoned. All that is left are a few old houses and buildings and a new golf course. Investigations have uncovered paranormal activity in the woods behind the golf course. Fairies and will-o'-the-wisp abound in the trees and lush greenery. The fairies appear at twilight with the lights and they dance through the trees. The lights often burn brightly and as one comes closer to them, both they and the fairies disappear.

Proctor House
Proctorville: Old 64 east of Marengo
(and Proctor House Cemetery; aka Woods Cemetery)

This house was built by William Proctor in 1832. He operated a stage coach stop, store and post office here. The Crawford County Historical Society currently owns and maintains the building.

Visitors report pokes by unseen fingers. One volunteer remembers hearing children giggling on the second floor. When she went to investigate, she found one of the upper rooms in disarray. She left to get another volunteer and when she returned, the room was back to its proper state.

Shoe Tree
Milltown: 3826 S. Devils Hollow Rd.

Stories abound about this shoe tree that has been around for at least 60 years. Supposedly Larry Bird has a pair of shoes hanging from the tree. It was burned by lightening a few years ago. Maxine McFelea Archibald, who owns Maxine's Market in Milltown made signs to direct people to the location. However, nothing on the signs indicate the paranormal activity. Shadow figures and a child lit by a bright light walk down the road near the tree.

Wyandotte Caves
Marengo: Harrison-Crawford State Forest (off IN 462)

Henry Rothrock hired three men to dig trenches so visitors could come to the caves. He only saw the men except on payday. Andrew, Henry's 19 year old son, would spend hours exploring the caves. Work was progressing nicely and a tour guide decided to explore up to where they'd finished. He found a printing press for counterfeiting. The sheriff caught two of the three men, but the third holed up in the caves. After weeks of armed guarding, they assumed he was dead. Some people believe that the voices heard come from at least one of the men from the counterfeiting ring.

Years later, two men decided to explore the caves. They went very far into the caves and their oil lamp was extinguished by water. For three days they tried to figure a way out. Suddenly, a bright light shone in front of them and a young man guided them out. The men were so grateful they vowed to return and give him some sort of present. When they did return, they found no one at the cave. They went to the Rothrock home, which was the nearest home and asked about the young man. Rothrock told them that his son had been diagnosed with histoplasmosis- a condition that occurs from excessive exposure to bat droppings. Rothrock explained that Andrew couldn't be the person that helped them as he died in the cave when Rothrock took him in one last time. However, he changed his mind when the men pointed to a picture of his son, taken shortly before his death, and identified him. The light is still seen from time to time at the caves.

Wyandotte Woods Cemetery
Marengo: Harrison-Crawford State Forest (off IN 462)

The gate to the cemetery is known to hit visitors as they enter or exit. Campers and investigators report a dark figure jogging through the woods at night.

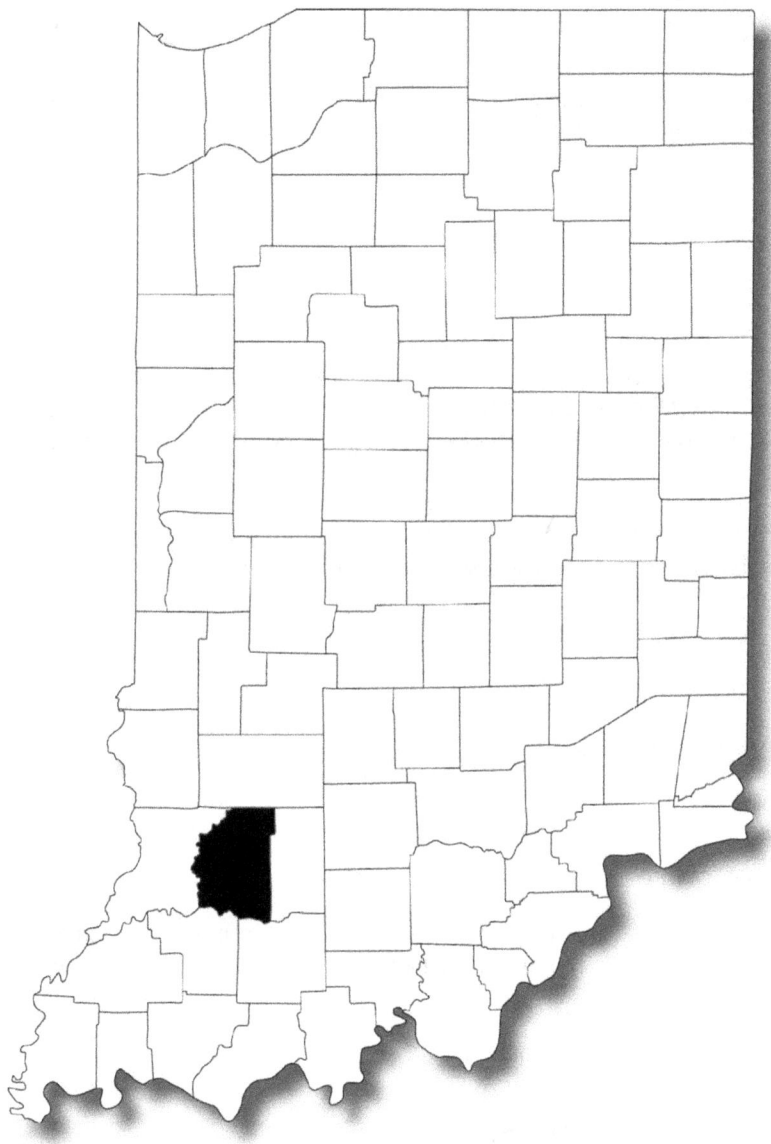

DAVIESS COUNTY

Alfordsville High School
Alfordsville: Unknown

Alfordsville doesn't have a school. Unless it is another school in the area or a school that burned down some time ago, the story of kids reported playing in a gym at night is pure legend.

Blue Hole
Washington: East of CR N300W (Oak Grove Rd.) along the railroad tracks about 1.25 miles west of town

Created during the flood of 1875, it remained quiet until March 27, 1913 when the Baltimore and Ohio work train moved the trestle that went over the blue hole. Four of the six men in Locomotive #401 died in the water. Within a half hour of this accident, the bridge over the West Fork of the White River collapsed leaving a total of 20 men trapped between the two bridges. On April 6, 1913 rescue crews found Locomotive #401. In Oak Grove Cemetery, a marker commemorates this event.

The Blue Hole is said to be bottomless, although some people believe it has a quicksand bottom. Today many people hear screams and cries for help coming from the area in which the accidents occurred.

Fairview Cemetery
Elnora: Off of SR 57 on CR 1500N

There are reports of several glowing tombstones.

Private Home
Alfordsville: Outside of town on Sugar Creek

A man killed his entire family and was found dead two days later. It appeared as if someone came back and killed him. Speculation is that the ghosts of his whole family came back to murder him. The house is full of cold spots even in the heat of summer.

William Hackler Farm
Odon: Home torn down by former owners

In 1941 the Hackler family experienced 28 random fires. They started from walls, a mattress, books, calendars, and other places. In one three hour period, there were nine separate fires. Firefighters from two communities waited to extinguish the flames. The house had neither electricity nor open flames to ignite them. During the time of the fire, the family's whereabouts was monitored. Traveler's Insurance Company paid for the damages stating they covered fires even of "supernatural origin".

DEARBORN COUNTY

Greendale Cemetery

Lawrenceburg: Greendale Cemetery Association is across the street from the cemetery at 886 Nowlin Ave.

Milk white and grey figures walk by the Tebbs family graves. Visitors feel watched, cold and uneasy.

Guilford Park

Guilford: SW of SR 1 off of Main St. (York St.)

(Note: This location is largely credited to Sunman, Indiana, but Guilford Park is in Guilford, Indiana)

A woman was hit by train and knocked into creek next to the tracks. Investigators were unable to get her out of the creek because it started to rain. Her body was washed away and never found. Visitors hear her horrific cries and the sound of impact from the train.

Laughery Creek Road

Dearborn County: Laughery Creek Rd. is between SR56 (Ohio Scenic Byway) and SR 262

In 1941 Harvey Sellars discovered the body of his neighbor, Johnston Agrue and his eleven year old granddaughter, Mary Elizabeth in the barn. When authorities arrived, they found Mrs. Agrue in the kitchen-dead. A son, Leo, was later found dead on a hillside and his brother, William was found shot in the back near Wilson School House. A son-in-law, Virginius "Dink" Carter was held for questioning. Later, he admitted to having dinner with the family, arguing with the sons and shooting the family. In 1942 he was eventually executed by electrocution at Michigan City.

From the time of the family's death, the area has been disturbed by their residual haunting. Twenty-eight years later, the Agrue house burned to the ground. Laughery Creek Rd. remains haunted.

Lesko Park

Aurora: SR 56

Mary Enzweiler drowned herself in the river on January 31, 2007. She cries and walks toward the river from the park.

Riverview Cemetery

Aurora: 3635 E. Laughery Creek Rd.

(See Laughery Creek Road, Dearborn County, Dearborn Co.)

Virginius "Dink" Carter killed the Argue family and is buried here. His spirit is seen reenacting the murders. He is buried less than 100 feet from where he shot two of the family members.

Whiskey's Restaurant
Lawrenceburg: 334 E. Front St.

This family owned restaurant was originally two houses and later a button factory. One of the women who lived in the home now haunts the Malt Room. The staff feels apron strings tugged and smells the scent of perfume in the back of the restaurant when no one is around.

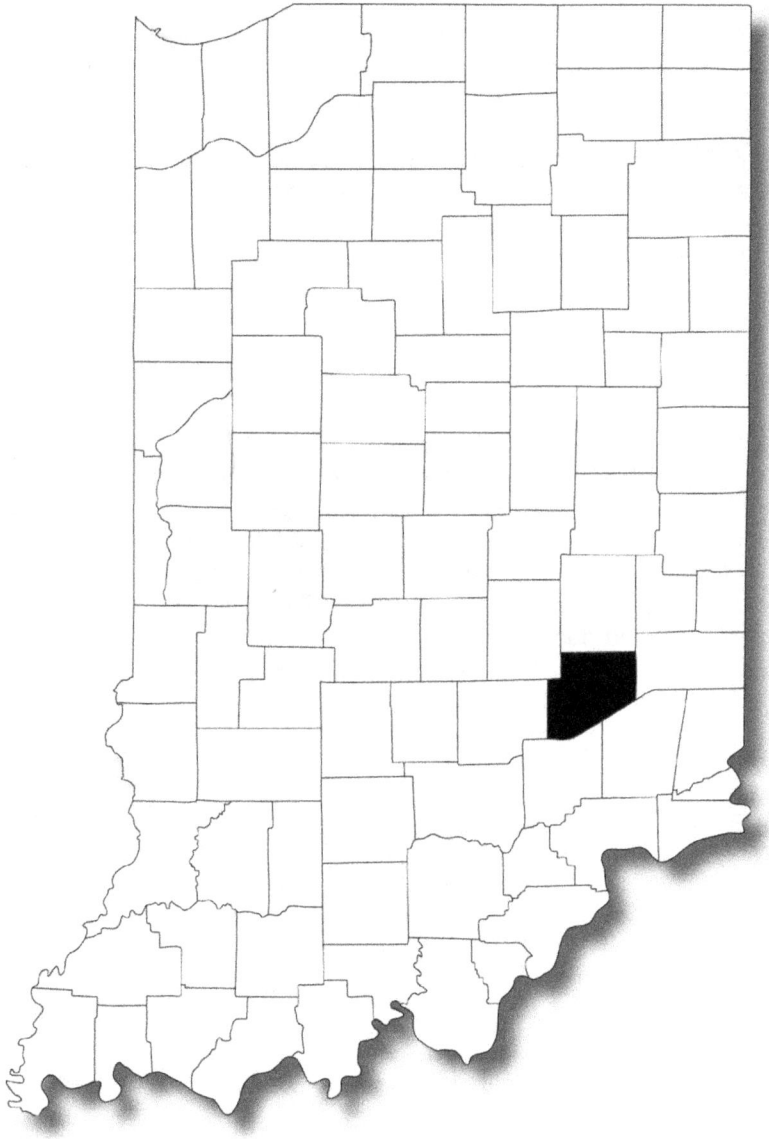

DECATUR COUNTY

Billings School

Greensburg: 314 W. Washington St. Old West End School has been razed.
(property housed Old West End School)
(Note: Now the area is a parking lot and has a building that houses city offices.)

The school was built in 1863. Later a mechanic died in the building. For many years, children lived in fear of being sent to the basement for punishment. They all knew the man continued to prowl the area. Some believe this ghost left when the Billings School was built in place of the Old West End School. Some staff and visitors believe the mechanic still roams the halls. A strange man dressed in work clothes walks in several halls. Visitors hear phantom footsteps.

Greensburg Courthouse

Greensburg: 150 Courthouse Sq.

Many staff and visitors to the courthouse feel the presence of a man. Other staff members working late at night experience breezes passing them or being touched by the spirit. In the basement, an ashtray moves on its own. The staff hears thuds and bumps around the stairway to the basement. In 1895 a janitor, Jack Thompson, was found dead on the stairs leading to the basement. Other people feel that the spirit may be a man who was hanged in 1879 by a mob, a block away. Another spirit has been seen on the second floor of the courthouse. A gentle looking woman in 1920s clothing has been seen sitting by several of the windows in the courthouse. When asked by staff if they can help her, she smiles, shakes her head sadly and disappears.

New Point Bridge

Greensburg: SR 46 (E Main St.) as you leave Greensburg

Like many bridges in Indiana, this bridge has a man encased in cement within a bridge support. He waves a lantern at night.

Sandusky Bridge

Greensburg: SR 3 just south of CR W680N

Like many bridges in Indiana, this bridge has a man encased in cement within a bridge support. He waves a lantern at night.

Scheidler Brothers Decorating

Greensburg: 318 S. East St.
(See South Park Cemetery entry, Greensburg, Decautur Co.)

Visitors and staff feel a presence in the building. Some speculate this presence may be connected to the South Park Cemetery ghost.

South Park Cemetery
Greensburg: On East St., south of E. McKee St. shortly before South Park Cemetery

On the historic stone bridge over Gas Creek, a well dressed man in a long silk top coat, and high silk hat appears to visitors. Sometimes they speak in passing to each other, but when people turn back to see the man again, they find he's disappeared. People speculate that this ghost could be President Lincoln visiting South Park Cemetery and Soldier's Circle. Activity usually happens at night, on foggy, cold nights, but also occurs (albeit less frequently) during the day.

Letts (town)

A baby is seen crawling and crying for its mother.

New Harris City (town)

A farmer is seen walking his bulls in the fields.

Old Railroad Bridge over Flat Rock River
St. Paul: Railroad tracks go next to E. Washington St. go SE over bridge

A man fell from the bridge during construction and died. A lantern moves back and forth on the bridge. Visitors also hear moans.

DUBOIS
COUNTY

Devil's Road
Jasper: CR N175E off CR E300N

Legend says that a bus full of children was hit by a train, killing everyone but the driver. The driver, overcome with grief, eventually killed himself. The children visit the spot regularly. When you park your car on the tracks and put your car in neutral, the kids push you off the tracks. Another male apparition walks toward your car with a lantern and disappears. Some investigators speculate that this figure is the bus driver trying to find any survivors of the crash.

Merkley Family Home
Jasper: E Schnellville Rd. Between Jasper (CR S300E) and CR S400E

A few miles from Jasper a farm boasts a haunted barn and grain shed. One visitor smelled pipe smoke and perfume. Numerous items have been thrown at people, and there are knocks on the door when no one is around. The farm also has a ghost of a little girl who likes to play with other children. She is about seven years old, appears as a solid figure, and loves to make noise- especially if it keeps you awake! The story indicates a little girl died in the pond on the farm near a former Native American village. Drivers have accidents and hit a lot of deer along the road in front of the farm.Deer or drivers bolt after seeing the Native Americans walking along the road. At the creek behind the farm, two boys drowned and at night you can hear them splashing. Several investigators have captured orbs and EVPs of splashes in the water.

Shiloh Church
Jasper: 1971 W. SR 56

The church burned, killing several people. Their spirits haunt the church. Many times on clear nights, the sounds of wailing, screams and even singing of hymns is heard.

St. Anthony Home
St. Anthony: SR 64 and S. St. Anthony Rd.

A family of nine people was in a car that stalled on the railroad tracks. Six of the people died when a train hit them. The house across from the railroad tracks is now home to the ghost of a little girl and an older woman. Objects move around the home and visitors hear noises in rooms when no one is in them. Some visitors to the home are pushed or kicked down the stairs.

FLOYD
COUNTY

1311 E. Elm Street
New Albany: 1311 E. Elm St.

Children sing "Ring around the Rosie" in the kitchen. A little girl in the upstairs windows look out at the street. A strange man pour buckets of liquid into unseen containers. Another man in suspenders paces the living room and walks through walls.

1600 Block of Oak Street
New Albany: 1600 Block of Oak St. Seventh house on right.

Home has many ghosts including a child, who played ball with visitors by rolling a ball into various rooms. The woman who owned the home died of a heart attack in 1995 and is said to be seen looking out of the windows at many times of the day.

Budd Road Cemetery
Blunk: *(Shively, community of Buchanan- near New Albany)*: Knob Rd. and Budd Road

White, foggy masses are seen in the cemetery. Sometimes the masses come into yards and homes.

Captain Frank's Tomb
Elizabeth: Off River Rd. SE. Parking provided. You'll have to walk up to the tomb.

Captain Francis "Frank" McHarry was a successful riverboat businessman. In the 1850s he turned to ferryboats. When he noticed the animals and people he transported were upset by the riverboat wakes, he became bitter. His vertical tomb is rumored to be built so he can overlook the river, and possibly curse the boats going by. Visitors have captured orbs and some investigators report seeing a shadow figure skulking around the tomb.

Culbertson Mansion (State Historic Site)
New Albany: 914 E. Main St.
(See Mansion at River Walk, New Albany, Floyd Co.)

This home was built by William S. Culbertson in 1867 at a cost of $120,000. Built in the French Second-Empire style, it contains hand-painted ceilings, rosewood, marble and crystal.

On the third floor Culbertson's first wife walks the halls, supposedly because of her dislike of the new wife. Spirits have been sensed. The vacuum turns on and off on its own. The spirits like to put things like dried flowers on the floor to be swept up. The third floor where the children's rooms and ballroom are host other ghosts. The third floor staircase is haunted by an old woman with grey hair; she is seen at night and during the early part of the day. She is also seen through the house.

The twin's bedroom has a heavy sense of death and one staff worker who spend the night there smelled dead fish around the bed in the twins room. When she asked that the smell go away, it did. The private parlor holds the remnants of harsh words spoken about the Civil War. Many times people have heard men arguing in this room.

Some tour guides have admitted the spirits are angry because they don't like people walking through their home.

Mansion at River Walk
New Albany: 704 E. Main St.
(A Culbertson Family Mansion)
(See Culbertson Mansion, New Albany, Floyd Co.)

This home was built by William S. Culbertson in for widows of wars and other tragedies. It mirrors the Culbertson Mansion State Site.

A woman named Roberta, a former owner, haunts the house. On the back second floor veranda, solid forms of women and captains are seen chatting. In the autopsy room, a strange mix of energy is felt. Visitors have seen orbs in the home, especially the in autopsy room. The basement of the building is home to several wispy grey figures that glide from room to room. Visitors report hearing knocking on their doors during the day. The widow's meal bell rings for no reason and the phone rings when no one is on the line. The front gate opens and closes on its own.

New Albany National Cemetery
New Albany: 121 W. Spring St.

Colored orbs float through the cemetery. Soldiers from all time periods are also seen in the cemetery. An EVP saying "got a light?" was captured.

Pine View Elementary
New Albany: 2524 Corydon Pike

J.R. Hays died when his bike hit a truck on Corydon Pike. At 8:47pm, you will hear his bike tires, and the truck slam on its brakes. The truck appears at the stop sign. Visitors have also reported hearing voices and sirens and someone saying "Why don't you help? Help me!"

FRANKLIN COUNTY

Brookville Inn
Brookville: 1049 Main St.

The inn was built in the early 1900s as a private residence. According to several visitors the Delft Blue room is active. A small child plays with jacks inside and outside the room.

Metamora (town)
Metamora: US 52 near IN 229

Metamora is an early canal town with an operating grist mill, wooden aqueduct and restored lock. The whole town has several spirits; some seem to move from location to location.

Metamora Inn
Metamora: 19049 Wynn St.

The inn was built in the 1850s. According to several visitors Clara's room is home to spirit activity. A man with loud work boots is seen pacing the room. A woman has been seen sitting in the Suite room looking out the window.

Thorpe Country House Inn
Metamora: 19049 Clayborne St.

Built between in 1840-1860, the inn is listed on the National Register of Historic Places. Investigators sense a comforting presence of a woman smelling of lavender and cinnamon.

White Hall Tavern
Laurel: Baltimore and Franklin Streets

The house was built prior to 1832 and was famous for hospitality and good food. Squire Isaac Clements did not allow hard liquor at the establishment. A newborn baby and its mother, who waiting for her husband to return, died shortly after childbirth. Her shushing noises to her baby are heard periodically. Guests hear a wailing baby too.

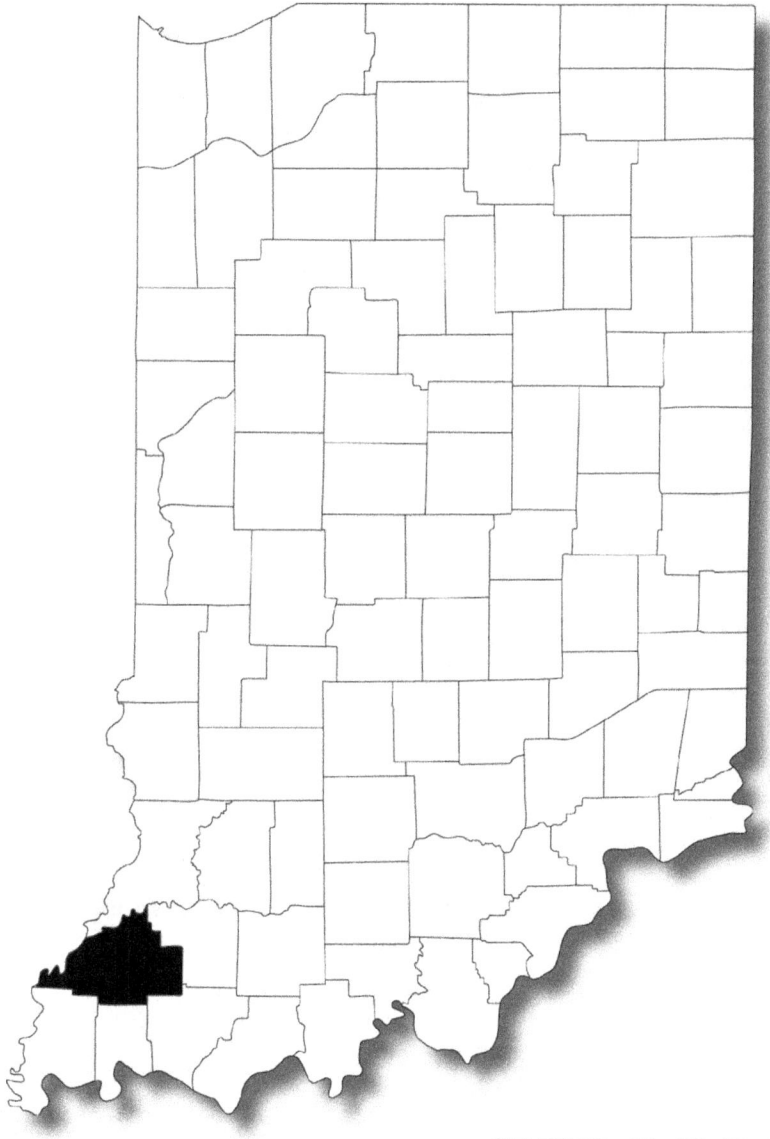

GIBSON COUNTY

Blackfoot Cemetery
Oakland City: Off IN 61 at CR 900
(aka Old Burial Grounds)

Investigators captured orbs and the figure of a woman. One sensitive was possessed by the spirit of a man who died in a car accident. A person was thrown from a vehicle for stating disbelief in the hauntings.

Bulldog Bridge
Princeton: Head east out of Princeton on the main road

Several people hung themselves from the bridge. One man was found dead in his car, the doors were locked and windows up. Visitors feel cold spots in the summer. Some people hear growling from nearby cornfields. A woman in white lures you under the bridge. She disappears into the water.

Fairfield Inn
Princeton: 2828 Dixon St.

Guests have uneasy feelings, and experience violent shaking and convulsing, and feelings of being ill. The apparition of an evil woman seen in rooms.

Gibson County Courthouse
Princeton: 101 N. Main St.

Built in 1884, this courthouse is a great example of Romanesque Revival. A Greek cross design is made from the four towers and four entries. The building also has a widow's walk. Black walnut woodwork, oak flooring, mosaic tiles and plaster reliefs have survived for over 120 years.

Visitors hear footsteps, and yelling. They are touched by unseen hands. One visitor swears she heard a man growl "I'll get even with you!" and a felt cold breeze pass her although she was alone in the corridor.

Lyles Station
Princeton: Intersection of Lyles Station Road and CR 500 W

Founded by Joshua Lyles in the mid-1800s, this structure is part of one of the last remaining African American settlements in Indiana. Visitors can see the type of schooling children would have received in the early 1900s. Visitors and staff hear footsteps in the building. One visitor, who was intently looking at an exhibit in one of the rooms, had a conversation with a bodiless voice. When she raised her head to look at the person, no one was around her.

Oakland City University–Cochram Hall
Oakland City: 627 W. Oak St.
(aka Oakland City College)

Lucretia, the wife of Col. William Cochram (founder of the college), hung herself in the upstairs tower. Witnesses have seen the doors open and shut and have seen an orange glow from the upper windows. Pink and orange lights are also observed.

GREENE COUNTY

Burcham Ford

Bloomfield: Although this is unverified, this location is supposed to be on CR 150S west of CR250S

A warrior stole a ham and the settler shot here. The Indian was buried out of fear of retribution. He was buried in the ford of Burcham Branch. Some nights he comes out of the water brandishing his tomahawk. People report feeling a breeze when he is around and hearing his war cry.

Fairview Cemetery

Linton: Take Fairview Rd. north out of Linton. It is a about a mile or two outside of town.

Polly Barnett was a derelict woman, she wandered around town trying to find her daughter, Sylvanie, who disappeared mysteriously. People of the town gave her shelter and food. People believed Sylvanie was murdered, presumably by a farmhand, although it was never proven. Her body found was never found. Polly died, without knowing the fate of her daughter. Before her death, she asked that her cat be allowed to roam to search for her daughter. The black cat is seen running through the cemetery during the day and night. It disappears when approached. The cemetery contains a memorial marker for Polly with a black cat on it.

Freeman City Hospital

Linton: 410 A St. NE

It was originally known as Freeman City Hospital after Job Freeman and his wife, who donated the land to build it. Started in June 1912, it was later renamed the Freeman Green County Hospital and later Greene County General Hospital. The hospital moved in April 1974 to its present Lone Tree Road location. Wendy's Restaurant bought part of the land and became established on the site on March 10, 1986.

Reports of footsteps and milk white, grey, and misty outlines of patients that died were seen roaming the halls prior to the hospitals relocation. One nurse reported having a conversation with a female patient who was dying- 30 minutes after she died.

After the relocation, an investigative team reported picking up visual forms and unintelligible sounds. Several pseudo-investigations of the current Wendy's and surrounding area have been done without obtaining proof of paranormal activity.

Ridgeport Cemetery

Ridgeport: SR 54 east of CR 725E

A log cabin used to sit in the woods behind the cemetery. Children who died of disease were buried in here. Today the sounds of crying and musical instruments can be heard.

White River
Newberry: White River
See Fairview Cemetery.

It's believed Sylvanie Barnett is the young girl seen walking along the river crying.

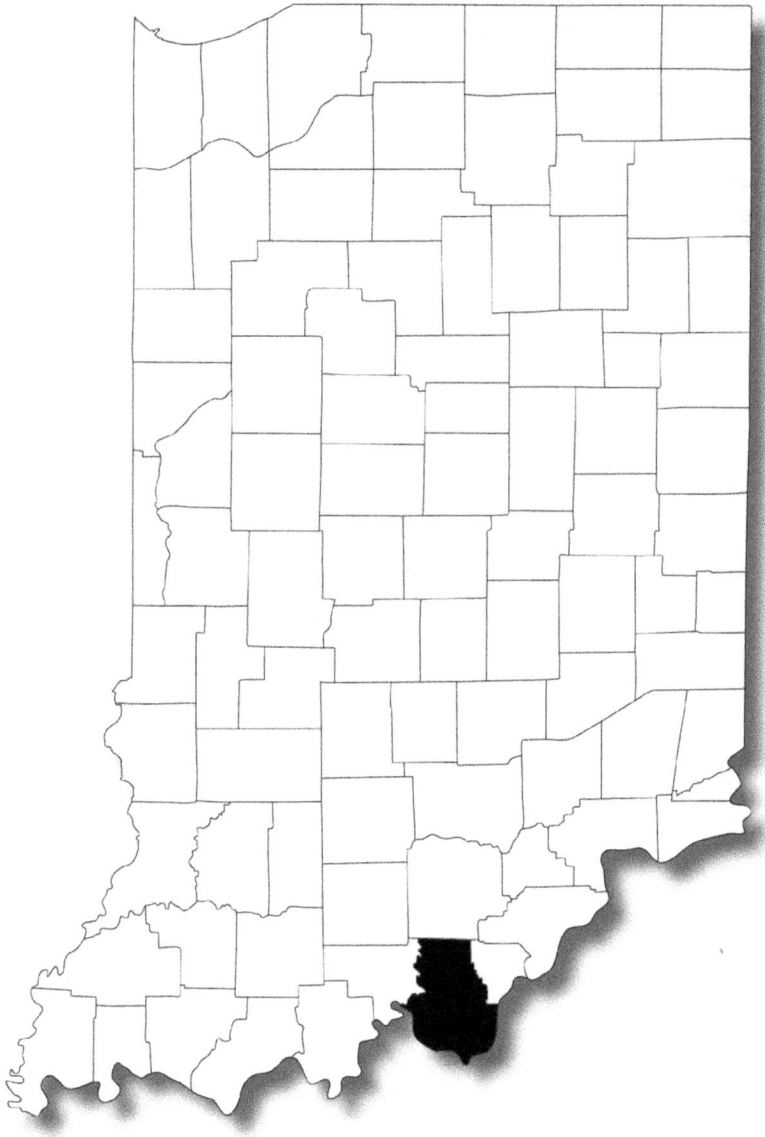

HARRISON
COUNTY

Battle of Corydon Memorial Park
Corydon: .5 miles from the center of Corydon on Old SR 135 South

On July 9, 1863, 450 members of the local home guard fought with Confederate Gen. John Hunt Morgan's Raiders on the south hill. After about thirty minutes, the men surrendered to Morgan and his 2,400 Calvary units, there were five casualties and 11 wounded. On one investigation, a psychic saw four translucent men in the woods, believed to be part of the military, surrounding the investigators. In all, there was a boy, a black man and two other men who could be farmers. Each figure was armed. They did not wear military uniforms, but wore military style hats and caps. During this display the temperature readings spiked hot and investigation equipment malfunctioned. EVPs were captured including the name Emma, who's believed to be the wife of one of the men.

Blue River
Corydon: Blue River

A woman in a canoe was decapitated when she ran into fishing line that was strung across the river. Many evenings she paddles her canoe in search of her head.

Corydon Town Square
Corydon: Town Square

Mary Bouchet was arrested and charged with murdering her child. She was hung in the town square. Her voice and cries are heard there today.

Dove's Nest
Corydon: Unknown

This location was a brothel in downtown Corydon. It is said to be haunted by several women who had either committed suicide or who had been killed by jealous customers.

Lickford Bridge and House
Harrison: Lickford Branch Rd.

The bridge was built in 1920 and rehabbed in 1989. In 2007, the bridge was closed and declared unsafe. A through truss bridge runs over Indian Creek on Lickford Branch Road.

Many stories about this area abound. The most famous is that of an evil Satan-worshiper who sacrificed his illegal slaves under the bridge. Some parts of the legend say he cut the slaves' throats himself with his long fingernails.

If you go to the bridge, he will appear from behind a tree and walk toward you. Some visitors have reported being punctured by his long nails. Other visitors said the handprints of slaves appear on your car. They say the slaves are trying to push your car off the bridge and onto the road to get you away from the man.

The Lickford house is next to the bridge. Supposedly Mr. Lickford went crazy and killed his family, burying them under the porch of the house. If you go into the house, he will throw objects at you. In pictures taken at the location, the family has appeared. Batteries have been drained and compasses refuse to work.

Ohio River

Maukport: Two miles west of Maukport on River Rd. (Maukport/New Amsterdam Rd.) where the road is very close to the river.
(aka Mauckport)

Pirates loved this area around the Ohio River. One night a boatman fell asleep and was ambushed by pirates, who severed his head. From that time, he's been seen headless, wandering the river beds west of Maukport.

JACKSON
COUNTY

191 W. Harrison Drive

Seymour: 191 W. Harrison Dr.

(aka Richard's House)

When a little boy named Richard died in the home, his parents planted a rosebush to remember him. When the parents moved, the new owner tried to get rid of the bush but couldn't. Every time they dug it up, it would return even bigger. The owner was eventfully successful. From that point, the bathtub in the home would drain when the plug was in place, clothing was displaced, and the television was operated by unseen hands. A picture fell from the wall and rolled to the television. Many noises were heard at night but nothing was ever found out of place. No figures were ever seen and the events seemed to abate when the person who dug the rose bushed up moved out.

County Road 275S and Guthrie Cemetery

Medora/Guthrie: CR 275S and Guthrie Cemetery

In 1861 a Civil War soldier , Aesop Wilson, Co. B, 22nd Inf., died of typhoid fever in a camp near Boonville, Missouri. His mother refused to bury him and for 12 years, she kept his sealed, charcoal-packed coffin in the hallway at the front of the house. Often she could be seen talking to her dead son and sewing by his side. In 1873 her husband, Creed Wilson had two spiritualists from Louisville come to the house to communicate with her son. They held a seance and supposedly she heard Aesop's voice say it was time. They buried him in the cedars north of their house on CR 275 S. Creed died two years later and was buried in the Leesville Cemetery. When his wife died a couple years later. The house remained vacant. In 1905 Aesop's last letter to his mother was found in the house. Eventually, Aesop's grave was moved because US 50 was ran through the area. It was moved to a "pasture" in the southeast part of Leesville or as some versions go, to the Leesville cemetery to be next to his father. Although legend claims that when the mother died, the people who took care of her estate buried Aesop's remains when they buried hers, we know that this is not true. The legend also says her ghost comes back to her home because she's mad that her son was buried. People in the area never wanted to go by the house; because they said they see white shimmering figures of the family in the house.

600 E. Tipton Street

Seymour: 600 E. Tipton St.

A Civil War soldier walks in this Papa John's Pizza restaurant. This hazy, transparent apparition never fully materializes. The store next door is reported to have thuds, bumps and voices come from it, even when no one is renting it.

Azalia Bridge

Seymour: US 31 north out of Seymour turn right at Azalia. It's the first bridge.

Several legends surround this bridge. First, a couple who went to a dance were killed on the bridge. If you drive to the bridge and honk your horn, the couple will appear and ask for a ride. When you give them a ride, they will get out before you can get them to their location. Screams have also been associated with this bridge.

Another legend involves a woman who was run out of town because she was pregnant. She stayed at the bridge and eventually threw her baby off the bridge and killed herself. Some people say you can hear the baby crying or see it crawling on the bridge. Other visitors claim if you visit the bridge after midnight, that the woman will possess your body and try to drive you off the bridge. Yet another story involves a little girl who was walking home being hit by a car. If you stop on the bridge at midnight she will get in the car, but as you leave the bridge she disappears.

A final story involves a farmer who caught his wife cheating on him, so he cut off her head. She roams around the bridge looking for her head. It's said if you see this white transparent woman that you too will die without your head.

The Coffins
Bobtown: CR 500 E
(aka The Flats, The Bottoms)

The legend states that in the late 1950s or early 1960s a policeman was called to a party at the Coffins. The kids killed him and put him in a tree. He wasn't found and he tree grew around him. Some people claim at night you can see his ghost roaming around, and see him peer down at you from the tree.

Another dubious legend claims that the poorhouses and insane asylums would bury their dead in shallow graves rather than pay for a funeral (and because experiments were conducted on the individuals (see Central State). The coffins would pop up during times of high water and they would float down the creek.

Babies are heard crying. Sometimes the cry of a wolf is heard. The ghosts of Native Americans are seen in the trees surrounding the area. Other apparitions include a boy, a moaning woman, and three white spirits that travelled in a pack around the coffins area.

Cortland Bridge
Cortland: On IN 258 between N CR 425E and Vehslage Rd. Some accounts state it is the pool to the north of IN 258 closer to Cortland and others believe it is the one to the south of IN 258 at the same location. Still others believe it is a single pool on the south side of IN 258 farther to the east and closer to Vehslage Rd.

On one side of the road is a stream. On the other is a large lake. Allegedly this lake is bottomless. Many people have gone into the lake and have never resurfaced. Some people believe the lake's bottom is full of quicksand. Geological surveys show another lake under the current lake.

Crothersville City Cemetery
Seymour: Take Main St. past S. Bethany Rd. Take first right road. Cemetery on left.

A statue in the cemetery is said to shake your hand. Other visitors say that it isn't the statue, but the ghost of a banker who died in the late 1800s after he bankrupted the bank he worked for.

Earl D. Prout Auditorium

Seymour: 1350 W. 2nd St.

In one of the homes that used to be at the site, a woman killed her daughter. Visitors, staff, and students hear a girl playing. Strange voices are heard in the auditorium. Some of the voices have been captured on recordings but cannot be made out. A little girl in blue skips through the room.

Freeman Field

Seymour: Includes the Freeman Field Airport and industrial park. (Near "A" Ave)

Part of the legend is that a Horten (German fighter plane) is buried at the field. Two Hortens flew in one day, but only one left. Supposedly it was buried, although no one can prove that conclusively. Today, ghosts of the workers at the field are seen. Sometimes they will talk to you as if you are part of their time period. Other times, they pass you without saying a word or acknowledging you.

Haunted Railroad Tracks

Seymour: From Seymour you take IN 11 south to 100 S. Wischmeier. Turn right on to 100 S. Wischmeier and take that road all the way till you see a dead end sign. Keep going straight it turns into a gravel road. Keep going then you'll see the rail road tracks.

The legend states that a carload of people were killed by an oncoming train. Several suicides have occurred in this location. If you use your cell phones or radios, strange noises come over them like old radio frequencies.

Interstate 65
Crothersville

A phantom Ford is seeing driving on I-65 for at least 40 years. It is sometimes seen on main roads. It always outruns the police and has no driver. One woman was unlucky enough to be stopped at a light with the vehicle and became very unnerved when the car's radio switched from commercials to hard rock. Additionally, motorists have reported being tailed by this vehicle.

Old Weddleville High School

Weddleville: SR 235 runs through Medora. The school is on old US 50 east of Medora. This school is currently undergoing preservation and will be available for rental through the Weddleville Cemetery Association.

This structure is over 150 years old and is believed to be the oldest remaining pre-Civil War school in Indiana. In more recent times visitors to the old school have heard children talking inside the building. They've heard writing as if on a slate or chalk board. Presumably teachers have asked students questions, and the unseen children have answered.

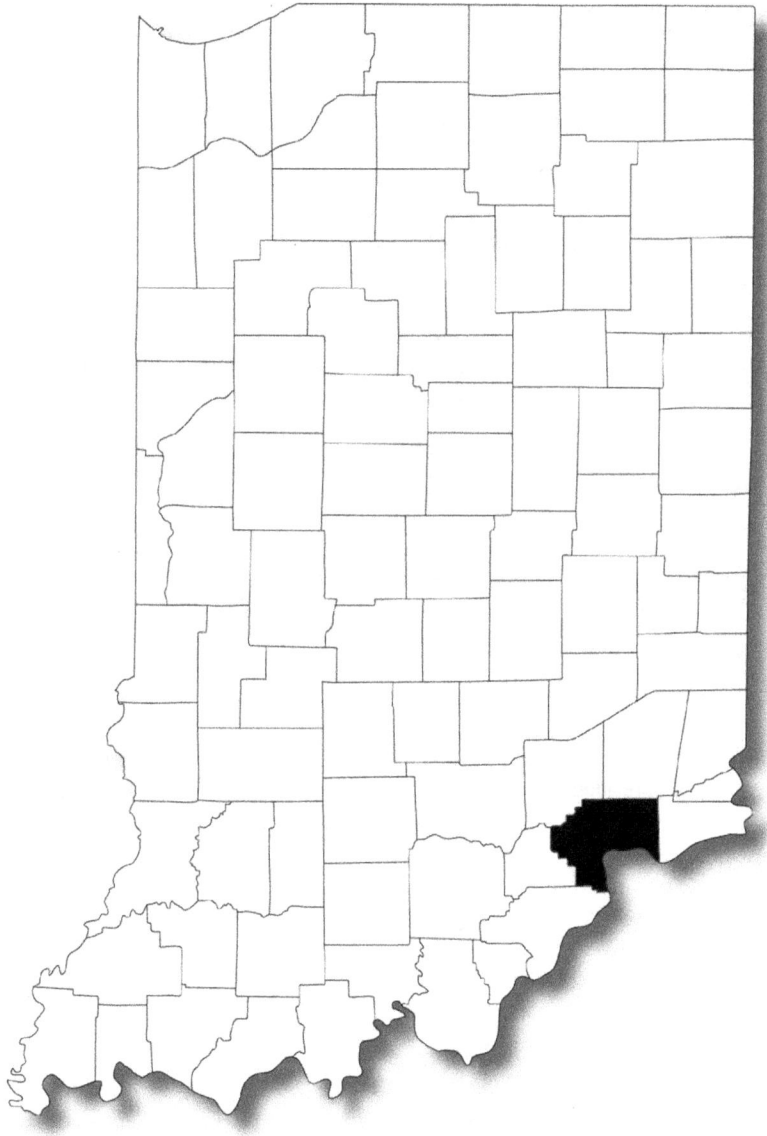

JEFFERSON COUNTY

American Legion Post 9
Madison: 707 Jefferson Street

(aka American Legion Home)

An old woman in black and a man in dress pants with suspenders haunt the basement. People report strange feelings, being touched and cold spots.

Big Creek, Fairmount, Baxter, Monroe, and St. Patrick's Cemeteries
Madison: State St. and Michigan Rd.

These cemeteries are at the same crossroads. Visitors have reported feeling ill, feelings of dread and feeling very sad in these connected cemeteries. Additionally, a little girl with long dark hair and black eyes walks through these cemeteries and sometimes follows visitors.

Clifty Falls State Park
Madison: 950 Cross Ave.

People hear moaning and see a woman near the walkway to the falls.

Clifty Village Mobile Home Park
Madison: Clifty Dr. (SR 62) & Chauncy Ln.

Items disappear. Pets in the residence seem sensitive to unseen spirits. Shadows shift through the wooded area to the south. Voices are heard calling names of residents and visitors.

East Splinter Ridge Road
Madison: East Splinter Ridge Rd.

Three small children, with a milk-white ghost dog are seen at various spots on this road.

Hanover Beach
Hanover: Off S. Riverbottom Rd.

A riverboat full of people sunk. A minister drowned while going for help. He appears on foggy nights at 2 a.m. No word on the fate of the others.

Hanover Cemetery
Hanover: Off W. First St. on Lowrey Ln.

Visitors have felt nauseous and cold. The legend is that Benjamin Bennett who was a student at Hanover College, drowned in the Ohio River. While his body was never found, but a tombstone was put in place for him.

Hanover College
Hanover: 359 E. LaGrange Rd.

Donner Residence Hall: A student committed suicide in the residence hall. Items move and moans and crying are heard.

Parker Auditorium: Dr. A.G. Parker, former President of the college haunts the auditorium. Visitors have seen him as a transparent and solid form. He is heard talking and he is also attributed to many odd sounds and missing items.

Hanover Nursing Center
Hanover: 410 W. LaGrange Rd.

A photo with a green mist has been reported as paranormal activity. Balloons mysteriously move about the nursing center. A piano plays on its own although no one is around. Activity increases before a resident dies.

Jefferson County Library
Madison: 420 W. Main St.

A ghost nicknamed Charlie rides the elevator in his wheelchair and strokes women's arms and legs. He lived at the location before it was a library and loved women.

King's Daughters' Hospital
Madison: 1 King's Daughters' Dr.

A lady in white haunts the second, third and fourth floors. She's been seen in the early morning from 2am-6am. On the fourth floor, a little boy rolls a ball down the hallways at night. Workers have seen the ball and have rolled it back to him.

Lanier Mansion
Madison: 601 W. 1st St.

The youngest Lanier son, who drowned in the Ohio River, is seen walking through town, from the river to the house and on the grounds. A ghost cat is seen and heard. In the children's room, the bed creaks as if someone is sitting on it and footsteps are heard running in the upper floor. The first and third floors are home to a lady in red who makes appearances toward the late afternoon. The third floor beds seem to be slept in as well; staff must remake them often. A puzzle that is kept there always looks as if someone has played with it. Voices are heard throughout the mansion. Doors that are bolted from the inside open on their own.

Little Doe Run Road Cemetery
Madison: E. Little Doe Run Rd.

Little Doe Run is allegedly haunted by a person named Flavius Bellamy.

Madison Country Club
Madison: Country Club Rd.

In 1842, this home was called the Hunter House. In the mid 1850s, the site was used as a fairground. During the Civil War, the home was used as a hospital, and after the war, it became Madison General Hospital. At one time, it served as the Indiana State Fairgrounds. Civil War soldiers walk the course. Chains rattle and Confederate soldiers are seen.

(Note: Country Club is closed but the grounds and building are used for private events)

Madison State Hospital
Madison: 711 Green Rd.
(aka Muskatatuck)

Orbs and noises are heard on the site.

(Note: This facility is still in operation, although many buildings have been closed/remodeled. Be respectful.)

Ohio Theater
Madison: 105 E. Main St.

The balcony is a hotbed of activity; orbs are seen and cold spots are felt. Two ghosts are said to haunt the building- a stagehand that fell from the balcony and a heartbroken chorus girl who killed herself by jumping from the balcony.

Springdale Cemetery
Madison: 5th St. and Suggett Dr.
(aka Cemetery at Hanging Rock Hill)

On Easter morning a statue of an angel cries blood.

Windrift Motel
Madison: Private residence. On Clifty Drive .5 miles before the entrance to Clifty Falls State Park

Shadow people and apparitions may be seen in the former hotel.

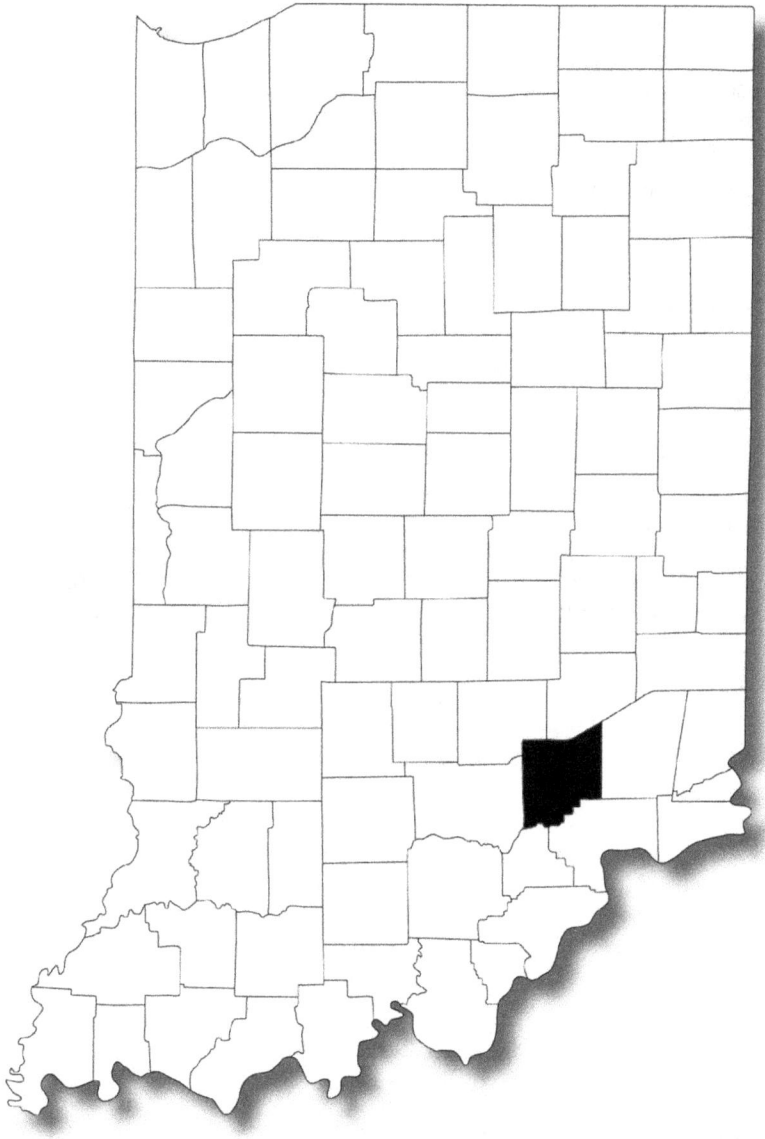

JENNINGS COUNTY

Baldwin Cemetery

Vernon: IN 25 to lane on left side that disappears into trees. Cemetery at end of lane.

Mary Smith sits by her grave crying. She was accused of being a witch. A man attacked and raped her. To cover his crime, he stabbed her to death. She's been seen at her grave in a bloody dress. Drops in temperature are reported in the old part of the cemetery, and voices are heard in the newer part. EVPs are frequently gathered. In one men's voices were captured saying "nothing" and "it wasn't my fault".

Commiskey (town)

Commiskey: South of Vernon on SR 3

Commiskey has gray mists, cold spots. Items will disappear and are returned elsewhere. Gray figures of a man and woman move about in the home. People have reported hearing their names spoken when no one is around.

Downtown Bed and Breakfast

North Vernon: 51 N Madison Ave

Once used as temporary housing for railroad men, this bed and breakfast now features several ghosts. Visitors have witnessed game of chess played by unseen hands. Footsteps walk down the hall and stairs day and night. Investigators have great success speaking with the spirits. At last count, 12 spirits inhabit the building. A couple of men said they died on the railroad, one in an explosion.

Jennings County Historical Society Museum

North Vernon: 134 E. Brown St.

In 1838, this former stage coach stop was home to Matthew Phillips, who drowned. Beds in the museum seem to be slept in. A child's footsteps are heard.

Muscatatuck Urban Training Center

Butlerville: CR 350 N and CR 475 E
(aka Muscatatuck State Developmental Center)

The Indiana Farm Colony was originally a working farm for disabled adult men. In 1925, the structure changed and more education was added to the residents' lives. When the institution became the Muscatatuck State School in 1941, the facility allowed women as well. At present the facility is used for Homeland Security Training.

Visitors report a bigfoot-esque creature at least seven feet tall.

Six Mile Cemetery
Hayden: South of W. Base Rd. on CR 610

A smallpox epidemic over 150 years ago killed the parents of the children, leaving many orphans. The town nurse tried to do her best but the disease spread to the children as well.

Ghostly figure of a woman nurse walks or runs across graveyard and stands at a fence near the road. Hear children crying and giggling. A gravestone in the shape of a chair moves on All Hallows Eve.

KNOX
COUNTY

Fort Knox II
Vincennes: 3500 N. Lower Fort Knox Road

This fort was actually called Fort Knox and the locals nicknamed it Fort Knox II. In 1803 it was built for $200. Many duels were fought here, most notably for desertion. In 1811, William Henry Harrison gathered his troops here before the Battle of Tippecanoe, where Native American's were heinously slaughtered. Karma, being the woman she is, saw to it that. Many of the troops died of their wounds upon their return to the fort.

The fort was disassembled a year later and it is now a state historic site. The ghosts of the dead soldiers and other slaughtered Native Americans haunt the grounds.

George Rogers Clark Memorial
Vincennes: South 2nd St.

As Indiana's oldest city, it is no wonder this area has its share of ghosts. Vortices and orbs have been reported in this beautiful structure dedicated to George Rodgers Clark, known for a brigadier general on the northwestern frontier during the Revolutionary War.

Otter Pond
Vincennes: Enter from Witterreid Ave.
(aka Otter Lake)

Donna Mariana Gonzales settled by the lake and fell in love with a local boy named Duffee. Her father wanted her to marry an older man in Mississippi. Instead, she took her life in Otter Lake where her beloved found her. Still, her cries can be heard. Sometimes her face peers at you from the water.

Purple Head Bridge
Vincennes: At the end of W Ferry Rd.
(aka Stangle's Bridge)

Many hangings occurred on this one lane bridge. One poor man tried to hang himself. His head was torn off, shooting blood onto the bridge. Visitors claim to have seen his purple head levitate toward, them and heard a scream as if someone is jumping off the bridge. One investigator was witness to this phenomenon and saw a spray of blood covering another investigator. When a picture was taken, the blood was not seen. A woman said goodbye to her lover here as he went off to war. They were to marry when he returned, but he was killed. Upon hearing the news of his death, she put her wedding dress on. At 11pm when she heard the train coming she stood on the track and was run over. Some believe they see James Jonston, a Revolutionary War hero, because he is unhappy people are on his land. Other stories indicate a battle between Native Americans and soldiers was fought here and several of them were killed in the water. Visitors say the head is also seen below the bridge through the planks.

Sigma Pi Fraternity

Vincennes: Old Wheatland Rd.

(aka Sigma Pi House; aka Shadowwood)

The national headquarters of the Sigma Pi Fraternity is haunted by ghost children. They are believed to be the children of the original owner, Col. Eugene Wharf. The Wharf makes an appearance from time to time.

Col. Wharf supported the Confederacy; and the area around his home was named Rebel Hill. Doors banging and footsteps have been heard. Cold spots manifest before people see the ghosts. Fogs and mists have also been reported in the home, usually accompanied by changes in temperature. A host of apparitions have been seen, ranging from men in Civil War uniforms to workmen and women.

Some of the oddest happenings have centered around objects being manipulated. People have poured hot coffee, only to have it go ice cold. Objects have moved across rooms and levitated. Lights turn on and off.

Ghost Hollow

Wheatland: 1 mile NE of Wheatland.

Now used for coal mining.

Lucy was a redhead who was born on a farm. When she got into arguments with her parents, she would take off on her horse. Once she and her father cooled down, the arguments would be forgotten the arguments would be forgotten. One day she said she'd been invited to a gathering of friends and she'd ride there. Her dad had a fit because she would be out late alone and he forbade her to go. She said she'd leave anyway they would never see her again and then she took off. When a storm started brewing she decided to go home. No one knows what really happened, but the next day her headless body was found on the path leading home. She is said to reenact her ride nightly, scaring people with her headless figure.

LAWRENCE COUNTY

818 14th Street
Bedford: 818 14th St.

Sylvan Moore had an affair with Atlee Osborn's wife. One night in 1928, Atlee, a stone carver, came home to find the two together. As Moore fled, Osborn followed, eventually beating him to death near 15th and H Street.

This scene is sometimes reenacted by a residual haunting.

Bedford
Bedford: Downtown Bedford

The night watchman patrolled the city streets, especially after a rash of break-ins were reported. In 1875 George Carney, a young Irishman, performed his duties with pride. One night he caught two men robbing the J.W. Mitchell drug store on the south side of the town square. Arthur Bissot and George Bachtel shot and killed Carney over postage stamps and less than one dollar in change. Green Hill Cemetery has a monument dedicated to Carney.

This scene is still reenacted by a residual haunting. Investigators have picked up unclear EVPs and have seen the members of the events and have heard the panting of someone running.

"I" Street
Bedford: The house is no longer standing, but it was near the current location of the Bedford Office Supply (1634 I St.)

In 1903, Susanna Ireland lived on I Street, earning her living as a dressmaker. On Labor Day 1903, her daughter ran to the Rippey Hotel and said her mother had shot herself. Investigators found Susanna neatly placed on the floor as though no struggle or evidence of the shooting had taken place. Cora Weeks, Susanna's daughter, and Cora's husband were charged with murder. According to the Lawrence County Historical Society, no court or newspapers exist that explain the outcome of Cora's charges. This was largely due to another murder that occurred- that of Sara Schafer.

Building owners in the area have reported seeing a woman from the early part of the 1900s looking as though she's working. One woman saw a white figure in a light colored dress with a pin cushion on her arm.

Lawrence County
Lawrence County: Johnson, Monroe, Lawrence and Brown County borders

A headless horseman is seen roaming the area riding on his horse.

Lawrence County Courthouse
Bedford: 916 15th St.

On the third floor of the courthouse, a woman watched her husband hanged on the north lawn. Her face froze in horror and is imprinted in the window.

Lawrence County Jail
Bedford: 1002 17th St.

In 1893 John Turley was in jail for shooting Lew Price, a train conductor. Drunk Turley had argued with Price over the train fare. As Price left the car, Turley shot him. A crew of 44 men stormed the jail and took Turley to an apple tree in front of the jail where they hung him.

Today, this jail is the Old Jail Art Center, where a host of different artistic media are taught and encouraged. Doors close without reason. Lights flicker off and on. Agonized wailing is also heard. Psychics say that there are many more spirits than Turley's in the building. A woman who was put in the cells for drunkenness and prostitution is said to have been taken advantage of by jail staff while in their care. Another man named Tinkey communicated that he was a long-time resident of the jail and he just didn't know where else to go after death.

Oscar Medaris Home
Bedford: Near 13th and "J" Streets

In 1918, Jack Taylor, a railroad foreman, was shot on the porch of the home where he boarded. Apparently Mr. Medaris was jealous of the attention he perceived Jack paid Mrs. Medaris. Jack pleaded not guilty by reason of insanity.

Investigators have captured the sound of two gunshots, the number fired in the killing. Others have reported seeing a man strolling up the walks of several homes in the area. Witnesses describe him as medium height and build, with a slouch cap and a weathered appearance.

Sheeks House
Mitchell: Where the New Albany and Salem Railroad crosses the Ohio at the MS Railroad.

Sheeks house was built in 1853. Doors would be found open when they had been securely latched. When nailed shut, doors would be found open with the nails rolling on the floor.

Spring Mill State Park
Mitchell: SR 60 three miles east of Mitchell

A female voice greets visitors as they enter the park. Other conversations with disembodied female voices occur within the park. The grist mill has had reports of several shape shifting entities. Photos of these entities have been captured by visitors and investigators. Investigators see a shadow figure in the mill at odd hours.

Stack Rock (in Wilson Park)
Bedford: 2107 Denson Ave. (you'll have to walk in the woods to see the rock.)

Limestone blocks make up this tall structure. Many paranormal investigators consider this location a portal to the other side. Investigators have recorded many EVPs and several instances of automatic writing exist.

Whispers Estates
Mitchell: 714 Warren St.

Legend has it that Dr. John and Jessie Gibbons had a foster daughter, and took care of other children. One child, Rachel, is said to have died in a fire in the home during Christmas 1912, although no proof of her existence has been found in local history. Five graves, although not confirmed by any reliable history, are said to be in the back yard. EVPs of Rachel and ghost children have been recorded. Apparitions of white, grey and black figures have been seen especially in the front parlor. EVP saying owners name when played backwards. Doors shake as though someone wanted entry into the building, yet no one was seen.

One story goes that a group a women spent the night in the house and after a few hours they were ready to leave. When one woman went home and told her husband that she didn't experience anything, he asked to listen to the EVP recordings she made. One one recording, as the women were talking about going up to the attic, her husband heard, "I'm waiting for you." on the recording.

Tunnelton Tunnel
Tunnelton: Between Tunnelton Rd. and Tunnelhill Rd.

A watchman fell asleep and didn't flag a train, to warn them of the sharp turn in the tunnel. The train crashed, killing everyone, including the night watchman. Since then, he's been swinging his lantern at midnight, trying to warn the train. The light is small at first, then it gets bigger as it swings from one end of the tunnel to the other. Some people have also witnessed seeing the train and the sound of a train in the tunnel, when there was no train present.

A man who was decapitated during its construction is seen in the tunnel carrying a lantern and his head. A legend that states a graveyard sits on top of the tunnel. During construction, the bodies fell into the tunnel. A family was killed when their wagon fell into the water. Now you can hear their screams.

Two guards would meet in the middle of the tunnel to switch sides during their shift. Once, one guard didn't see the other and went to tell him it was time to switch, he walked back to see if the other man was already on the other side. The missing guard was swinging from a noose. At night, you can see the hanged guard swinging in the tunnel.

Finally, a legend states if you write your name in the tunnel, when it is erased, you'll be dead-which seems to have happened to a number of folks. Countless stories of friends writing names only to see one disappear and that person dying have been told. It has even happened to people who move away. It seems once your name is in the tunnel, it will be erased when you die- no matter where or when that will be!

MARTIN COUNTY

409 Wood Street
Loogootee: 409 Wood St.

Reports of strange footsteps and loud, evil laughter have been reported for years at this location. Shadow figures are seen moving through the home when no one is home.

Brooks Bridge
Shoals: CR6 Brooks Bridge Rd. (east of CR31)

One fine June night, a woman jumped from the bridge. Investigators claim if you visit the bridge, you'll hear her running down the bridge and you'll feel cold air whoosh by. Another story claims a teenager killed herself by jumping off the bridge. The 17-year old was mad at her boyfriend and committed suicide. On the fifth of every month, if you visit the bridge, you will hear her run, jump and scream. Another version places the victim at middle age.

Clarke Cemetery
Martin State Forest / Loogootee: NW of US50 on Harvey Sutton Rd. just east of where Harvey Sutton Rd and Williams Rd. meet.
(aka Clark Cemetery)

Mists and orbs have been captured at this cemetery. One visitor reported visiting the site during the day and speaking with an old man who was repairing a stone. The visitor bade the man goodbye and turned to leave. She thought of another question and as she turned to ask him, she found the man had disappeared.

John F.Kennedy Gym
Loogootee: JFK Ave. between Vincennes and Riley Streets.

The basketball team used to run laps and practice here. One member tripped, fell, and died. At night you can hear the team running in the gym and you can hear the sound of someone walking and falling. On certain nights, you can see the blood stain where the boy died.

Haunted House
Alfordsville: Sugar Creek
A man strangled his family in this house. Rain, believed to be the tears of his family which fall throughout the house. The room the bodies were found in is always cold even if it is hot outside.

Hindostan Falls/ Hindostan Cemetery/ Sholts Cemetery
Hindostan Falls: South from Shoals on US50/150 to SR550, turn west and follow the signs. "The Rock" is the limestone ledge under the falls. Sholts Cemetery is between Brooks Bridge Rd. and Hindostan Falls on SR550. Hindostan Cemetery is on the SW corner of the town off SR550

This is a state fishing area, but once, it was a thriving town. In 1821 disease began sweeping the community and by 1828 the town was abandoned. Although it is unclear what type of disease took the lives of the population, speculation is that it was anything from smallpox (contracted from rats in cornmeal), yellow fever, or cholera. Many of the dead were buried in areas cemeteries; however, eventually an unknown mass grave was dug because of the tremendous amount of bodies accumulating. The majority of the townspeople eventually settled near Mount Pleasant. A local legend states that a woman who was driven out of town for being a witch cursed the town with a plague and that's why the town was destroyed. Today you can still see remnants of the old town, foundations can be found in the woods. Forgotten streets are also half covered in brush. According to locals, when the town moved to Mt. Pleasant, which was the county seat, and legend has it that the Hindostan Falls treasury, full of gold and silver was transferred to the town, but never actually made it there. This area is worth the trip with or without the ghosts because of its unique whirlpools. If you go to "The Rock" in Hindostan, you'll be able to see where the mill once stood. If the river is full, the falls are exquisite. Many visitors to the area have reported white outlines of men, women and children in the area, especially around Shoals Cemetery.

Loogootee Elementary East
Loogootee: 510 Church St.

When you look at the school, a red spot appears near the top of it. Some staff and students believe this spot appears because of a janitor that killed himself by hanging in the boy's bathroom. If you go into the bathrooms at night, you hear him pushing a mop bucked around the bathroom and hear his keys jangling. Some people also believe that the janitor used to bring his dog to work and on the second floor, sightings of a dog have been reported.

Peggy Holler
Shoals: Unknown

Peggy's husband cut her head off, and her headless ghost is often seen. Her husband is also heard calling "Peggy".

Pleasant Grove Cemetery
(aka Crane Cemetery)
Crane: On the grounds of Crane Naval Weapons Support Center. Visitors should enter through the Bloomington Gate (IN 45 and IN 58) or through the Crane Gate (IN 558,1 mile east of US 231).

This cemetery contains a glowing headstone. Enter the cemetery and turn your lights off and drive to the back. Once you are there look directly ahead of your car and you will see the headstone glowing. The glow will fade the longer you stay, but will cycle like a light house while you remain in the cemetery.

West Boggs Park
Loogootee: South of SR645E (1300E North) on US231 N

A phantom woman runs through the park at 10pm. She is the mother of a child who drowned. Late at night this woman screams while she tries to find her son. Investigators report having seen her in the lake at midnight with her son.

School House Hill
Pleasant Valley: School House Hill is off SR550 at the first western road south of SR550.

'Investigators have heard yells for help. One investigator was pushed down the hill on her way back from an investigation. She broke her wrist.

Shoals Community Junior-Senior High School
Shoals: 7900 US50

The school was constructed on a burial ground. Visitors hear unexplained tapping and rapping. Sports equipment has been known to become displaced. A strange watermark is seen to the south end of the gym. Doors close eerily on their own.

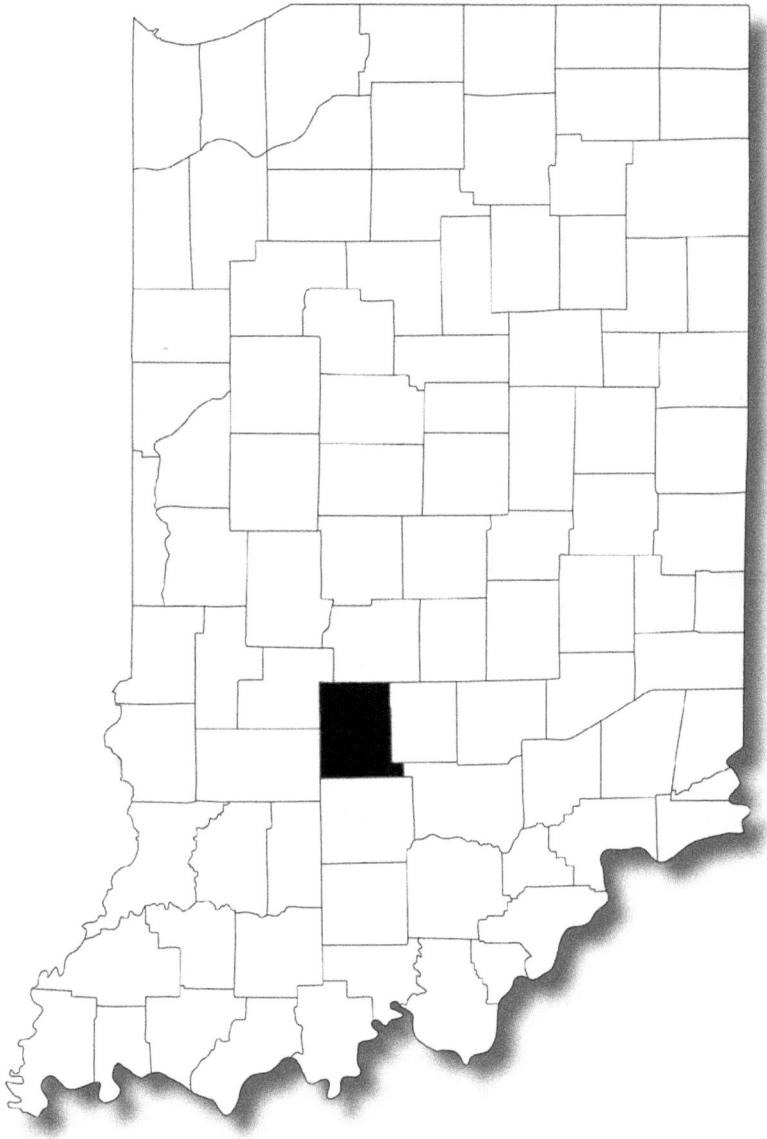

MONROE COUNTY

Binford Elementary
Bloomington: 2300 E. 2nd St.

A cloaked man walks through the school. Electrical problems plague the whole building. The man is believed to be a former school janitor who was killed by three students.

Buskirk Mansion
Bloomington: 520 N. Walnut St.
(aka Porticos)

This former home, now restaurant, was once part of the Underground Railroad. The first home predated the Civil War and this second structure was built in the 1890s. A girl's face is seen in a mirror. The sounds of children's laughter and running upstairs is heard in the dining room. Children are also seen and disappear quickly in other parts of the home. An upstairs dining room was found with broken dishes and glasses, and furniture overturned, yet no one in the restaurant had heard a sound. Wait staff sitting on the second floor couch jumped at the same time because they felt their backs burning. EVPs of children's voices have also been captured. Even the alarm company has monitored the sounds of children which have set off the alarms.

Hardin Ridge Recreation Area
Bloomington: SR446 in the Hoosier National Forrest.

A two legged upright creature is seen around the recreation area. It is reported as 5-6 feet tall weighing more than 200 lbs.

Indiana University- Arboretum
Bloomington: IU has a great map of its campus on its website.

A voice yells "Get off my home!" Shadows follow visitors until they leave. The legend states that a student died in the pond in the 1980s (or 1970s depending on the story teller) and the shadow figure of the person often stands by the pond.

Indiana University- Ballantine Hall
Bloomington: IU has a great map of its campus on its website.

Legend has it that a woman threw herself from a window when she found her boyfriend with another woman. This woman haunts the basement, where she saw her boyfriend. She is heard crying. The ghost of a janitor is heard rattling the doors to the rooms late at night. Doors on the 5th floor have been known to rattle and shake when no one is around. A janitor is also seen on this floor. On the 10th floor, orbs move and whisper in the air much to the surprise of visitors.

Indiana University- Burford Hall
Bloomington: IU has a great map of its campus on its website.

A woman ghost named Barb died of alcohol poisoning in the building. She vomits, flushes the toilet and cries. Whispers and items scraping on the walls and floors are heard.

Indiana University- The Career Center
Bloomington: IU has a great map of its campus on its website.
(aka Phi Kappa Tau)

The area where the Career Center stands is haunted by children who are said to be aborted from illegal operations in the early 1940s. Measured footsteps climb and descend the stairs. People report having been touched by unseen hands. Another legend has the builder killing himself shortly before the doctor moved in. A man seen washing his hands of blood has surprised people in the second floor bathroom. A female apparition fades from view in front of staffers and her cries echo the halls.

Indiana University - Cromwell Hall
Bloomington: IU has a great map of its campus on its website.

A white cross is sometimes seen on the 12th floor where a man committed suicide. A girl later died in the room. The man jumped from the west side in room 1221. Supposedly no one is allowed in the room.

Indiana University- Delta Tau Delta House
Bloomington: IU has a great map of its campus on its website.

A worker died during the construction of the house. He walks around the whole building and talks about the house.

Indiana University- Dunn Cemetery
Bloomington: IU has a great map of its campus on its website.

Moses Dunn deeded the land in 1855 to the Brewster sisters (who are buried there). Eventually the rest of the Dunn land was sold to IU. The sounds of babies crying are heard here.

Indiana University- Eigenmann Residence Center
Bloomington: IU has a great map of its campus on its website.

Suicides abound in this building and murders as well, most notably Susan Clements and Steven Molen, who were shot on the 14th floor by Andreas Drexler, who killed himself in his car. He apparently was stalking Susan. As a result, shadow figures, moving object and feelings such as severe melancholy and anger surge through visitors.

Indiana University- The Folklore Office
Bloomington: IU has a great map of its campus on its website.

Former chairman, Dr. Richard Dorson (1962-1981). After his death the lamp near the building used to stay on all the time. Dorson was seen leaning against it. He has also made appearances in the courtyard.

Indiana University- Goodbody Hall

Bloomington: IU has a great map of its campus on its website.

The sculpture of Donald Duck wearing a mortar board isn't the only odd thing about this building. A sobbing woman in white is seen crying on the steps inside the foyer.

Indiana University- Kelly School of Business

Bloomington: IU has a great map of its campus on its website.

In the large second floor lecture hall, footsteps and the sound of someone sitting in a fold-down chair are heard. A woman's laughter and screams are heard in the stairwells.

Indiana University- The Indiana Memorial Union

Bloomington: IU has a great map of its campus on its website.

Several human apparitions from suicides and a ghost dog are seen. In the old tower, happy laughter, footsteps and moving furniture are heard. A transparent man from the 1950s is seen under the painting of former IU President and Chancellor Herman B. Wells and in the Tree Suites. In the Tudor room, a picture of a child known as Jacob who died in a fire hangs on the wall. His ghost moves things on the tables in the dining halls at night. When his photo was removed, he trashed the room. In the Bryan Room, which used to be part of a hotel, a man turns on lights at night. He is believed to have been a guest that killed himself by jumping from the building and is scared of the dark.

Footsteps and laughter are reported. Lights turn off and on, In the Federal room, an unfinished painting of Mary Burne hangs. She seems to look at it from time to time and her perfume can be smelled, especially during 2-6am. In the Tree Suites, a man in a suit haunts the stairway. He supposedly killed himself in the building.

Indiana University - The Lily Library

Bloomington: IU has a great map of its campus on its website.

An apparition of a girl in blue is seen studying at one of the desks. She is usually seen close to closing time, or is seen from the windows after closing. Additionally, staff has heard conversations when no one is around. Items move from room to room. Some of the exhibits seem to bring spirits with them only to leave once the exhibit moves to a new location.

Indiana University- Maxwell Hall

Bloomington: IU has a great map of its campus on its website.

A figure of a young man glides through the halls at night, knocking on doors and laughing.

Indiana University-Memorial Stadium

Bloomington: IU has a great map of its campus on its website.

Michael Plume died here under mysterious circumstances. He was found hanging on the west side of the stadium. People believe he was killed because he was homosexual. Visitors and staff alike have seen him hanging in the building.

Indiana University-Old Cresent section

Bloomington: IU has a great map of its campus on its website.

The Lady in Black wears Victorian clothes and follows couples and men down the area of Third Steet, close to the sororities and fraterniies. Mostly seen around 3 am.

Indiana University-Reed Hall

Bloomington: IU has a great map of its campus on its website.

The Hall is named for Dr. Lyle and Nell Reed. An RA named Paula was under a lot of stress and killed herself in the 1980s. On the anniversary of her death, December 12th, you can hear her. She is also seen entering different rooms in the dorm. Another ghost is a woman with long black hair who is in a bloody nightgown. Her boyfriend was a medical student and hid her body in the campus tunnels. She is mostly seen wandering the halls, particularly the third floor.

Indiana University-Sigma Phi Epsilon

Bloomington: IU has a great map of its campus on its website.

Michael Pfang was enjoying a homecoming carnival at the edge of a street when a cannon on a float backfired. Pieces of it hit Michael and cut his head off. The fraternity believes he haunts their home as he was a pledge at the time of his death. Michael has been seen in the house, especially in the basement. According to records, his last duty had been to clean the basement. People hear running water, cleaning utensils and whistling. Also, items around the fraternity that go missing are blamed on Michael.

Indiana University-Student Building

Bloomington: IU has a great map of its campus on its website.

The Anthropology and Geography departments are haunted by a student who drowned in the pool that used to be in the building. However, according to records, this building never had a pool, so you be the judge.

Indiana University- Union Board Office

Bloomington: IU has a great map of its campus on its website.

Footsteps are frequently heard when no one is around.

Indiana University- Tunnels

Bloomington: Swain Hall, Third Street and the Union Building contain entrances.

The utility tunnels were constructed over 100 years ago and contain steam lines, voice and data communications, as well as chilled water and medium and high voltage. From Third Street to the Union Building to the Old Crescent, one can walk underground without being seen. These tunnels are extremely unsafe. They are hot (many people have suffered steam burns), full of sharp edges and full of cancer-causing asbestos. Not all of the tunnels have lighting and some parts are very small to the point that one has to crawl through them. Homeless people sometimes sleep in the tunnels.

A girl in a yellow nightgown haunts the tunnels. Legend states she was strangled by her boyfriend and dumped in the tunnel. She waits around looking for revenge.

Another legend is that an elephant died while en route through Indiana and animal activists stole it from IU (which was using it for research) and hid it.

Indiana University- Wright Quad

Bloomington: IU has a great map of its campus on its website.

A man broke up with his girlfriend. She was so heartbroken she killed herself. The Lady in Black is seen around the Quad at all hours.

Indiana University- Wells House

Bloomington: IU has a great map of its campus on its website.

In the early days of the university, the legend states a girl had to be kissed at the Wells House to become a coed. Today the legend states if you kiss a girl at the Wells House at midnight, you'll marry her.

Indiana University- Zeta Beta Tau

Bloomington: Corner of East 8th St. and N. Fess. Ave.
(razed)

In 1984 a former student and a fraternity member got into an argument. Zook, the former student, set fire to the Zeta Beta Tau house. Israel Edelman, who had been visiting, died from smoke inhalation. Zook was arrested and the fraternity moved to N. Jordan Ave. A memorial marks the spot of the former house. The smell of smoke and the ghost of a student have been reported on this road. Voices come from the plot of land, now used for gardening.

Kappa Delta Rho Fraternity
Bloomington: 1504 E. Third St.

A girl fell asleep and dreamed Stanley Rice, who had been killed in a car accident, came to her bloodied and disfigured. He came at her with a pick axe in the dream. The girl woke up but instead of being relieved, people heard hear scream, for the pickaxe was in her real life nightmare. When the people in the house came to her room, they saw the axe- which had been missing for six months.

Lake Weimer
Bloomington: Off W. Wapahani Rd.

The apparition of a woman searches for her husband in the lake. At times she walks along the water and other times she floats on the water.

Manann Cemetery
Bloomington: W. of Bowman Rd. on CR 300N

Once part of Miami Nation land, this cemetery has dancing red and green lights near the limestone obelisks. Footsteps are heard and the silencing of wildlife is also experienced.Strange knocks occur on cars and temperature drops are reported.Foul smells and chilling breezes are felt and smelt by investigators. Shadow people dart through the stones and stand at the edge of the cemetery as if keeping watch.Some investigators believe it is the work of Native Americans or even Civil War soldiers.

Matthews Mansion
Ellettsville: S. Edgewood Dr. and Edgewood Dr.

Voices and transparent apparitions of men, women and children are se

Paris Dunning House
Bloomington: 608 W. Third St.

Once part of the Underground Railroad, books fall from shelves, doors open and papers are heard shuffling. Some investigators believe that these noises come from slaves who were killed at the house.

Railroad Tracks
Oakville: Between Trailsend and Bluejay Dr.

The tracks at this location have largely been removed, however, several apparitions are supposed to be seen here. Former slaves who built the railroad track are one set of apparitions. An engineer with a lantern is another. Finally, a girl with a doll is seen running down the tracks. She falls and you hear a scream. She dissappears.

Raintree House

Bloomington: 111 and 112 North Bryan Avenue

The Raintree was built in 1882 for the Rogers family. In 1925 Agnes Wells purchased the house and later IU purchased it. Legend claims this was a stop on the Underground Railroad (which can't be true as it was built in 1882). Additionally a woman committed suicide by immersing herself in a vat of lye soap and ingesting it. EVPs here included mention of the basement, and a woman interacting with investigators in response to questions.

Rose Hill Cemetery

Bloomington: Entrance on Elm St. south of W. Kirkwood Ave.
(also part of Dodd's Cemetery)

Once time this cemetery was Bloomington's City Cemetery. Additionally, an old oak tree had the initials "GY" carved in it ("graveyard). Shadow figures, especially around the Evergreen Arbor. surprise and delight people. Hoagy Carmichael and several notable others are buried in this cemetery. Mists and orbs have been captured by investigators. One investigator was pushed onto the ground and couldn't get up. No amount of pulling from his friends could get him off the ground.

Bloomington-Step Cemetery

See Martinsville- Morgan County

OHIO
COUNTY

Cedar Hedge Cemetery
Ligionier: On First St. off west end of Downy St. (Behind Rising Sun High School)

Spirits follow visitors, and some claim they've blocked their exit out of the cemetery. These spirits have been in the form of full apparitions that have not seemed human, shape and size are too large. The spirits will follow you back to your car.

Empire House
Rising Sun: 114 S. Front St.

Built circa 1816 as a private home by Daniel Brown who operated a general store out of the front of the house. Later, he became a steamboat captain and helped build the fifth floor of the local Masonic Lodge. Various churches also held services in the building. The structure later served as several hotels including the Commodore Perry Inn. In 1885 the home became the Empire House (hotel and restaurant) and has remained so until today.

Several full solid apparitions of men have been seen in the home. One guest retired for the evening and was very surprised to see her door open and a man walk to the front of her room and disappear onto the veranda.

Mulberry Inn and Gardens
Rising Sun: 118 S. Mulberry St.

The Victorian Room has a ghost that likes to play with the plumbing. Several guests report water running in the middle of the night. One guest's shower turned on by itself shortly after she had checked in, brought her bags upstairs, and sat on the bed.

Old Mational Bank of Rising Sun
Rising Sun: 212 Main Street

Former occupant of upstairs apartment heard noises downstairs at all hours of the day and night. Many times, it sounded as though furniture was moved and scraped across floors. Twice the same occupant heard his name called and someone tapped the floor under his chair. When he spoke to the tenant downstairs, he found no one was supposed to have been in the building the previous day.

Another story is that a man came home and found his wife with another man. He strangled his wife and her lover with chains then disappeared. On the anniversary of the murder, he came back and saw they had been buried together. He was angry and was killed while driving. Some people believe a chain came through the window of his car and killed him. When they buried him, chain links, which signify life and ties to Earth, were included on his stone.

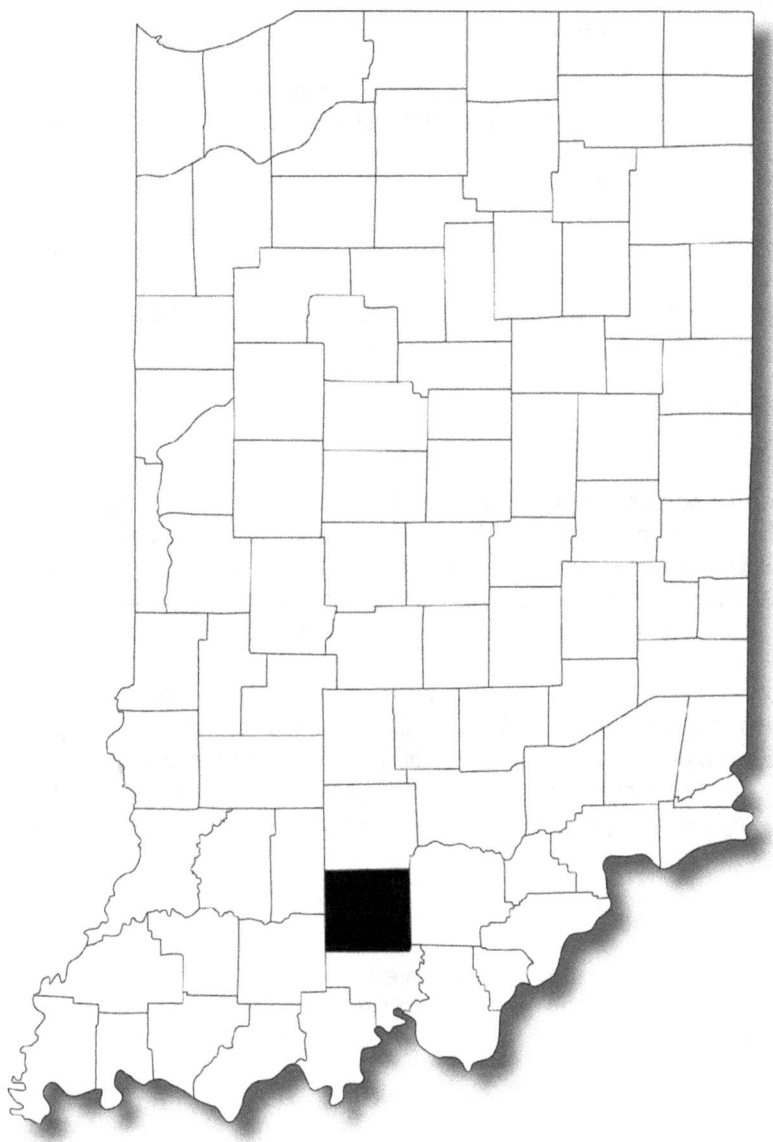

ORANGE
COUNTY

Bond's Chapel (Church/Cemetery)
Paoli: 8625 W. CR810N (West Baden)

A chain on a headstone grows a link each year. The stone was replaced but the chain reappears. The chain represents the love of a man in the Army and woman who waited for him. Their parents kept them from getting married before he shipped out, but his girlfriend waited. He was killed and brought back for burial. The girl didn't go to the funeral but stayed across the street. Today, the chain glows at night. Sometimes you will see a girl in black on other side of cemetery.

A similar story is that an illegal slave owner beat his slaves to death with a chain. One of the slave's wives put a curse on the slave owner. Every year after the slave owner's death a link of a chain is added to his grave, binding him to the graveyard. Legend has it if you touch the chain you will die/go insane/have tragedy in your life within seven years.

French Lick Springs Hotel
French Lick: 8670 W. SR56

This hotel was the place to see and be seen in its heyday. In the 1800s people came for all the sports and other amenities provided by the hotel. But they also came for the healing Pluto water of the springs. In the 1850s, it was a stop on the Underground Railroad. Dr. Bowles, the original owner, died in 1873 and Thomas Taggart bought the hotel. His family operated it well into the 1940s. After WWII, business declined and it was sold and restored by new owners. Most recently, after more years of struggle, it's been restored even further and has been renamed French Lick Spa Resort and Casino.

The hauntings at the location begin with Mr. Taggart. All the elevators are subject to him opening the doors or pressing buttons for people. Sometimes he's heard asking what floor- imagine the surprise of people when they realize he isn't there. The fifth floor, room 521 is host to ghosts who scatter clothing and change on the floor, and turn on the shower when no one is in the room. The sixth floor is host to shadow figures, and unseen presences. Misty figures reflected are in mirrors that make cleaning staff very uneasy. Staff and visitors have been touched, stroked, and one woman was kissed on the neck.

Horse Field
French Lick: Between Ames Chapel Rd. and Cave Quarry Rd. on SR150.
When a severe storm went through a horse field, two black horses and a black colt were killed. If you visit the fields when storms are nearby you are supposed to see the horses under the oak tree where they took shelter.

Mineral Springs Hotel
Paoli: 124 S Court St

This great old hotel has a wonderful buffet including chicken that tastes like it was fried in Crisco, and is served up hot and tasty. Paoli itself is a wonderful place to spend a day. Staff and visitors report hearing noises from the kitchens- pots and pans banging when no one is in the kitchen. A woman in 1910s clothing walks up the stairway. Sometimes she turns and smiles at visitors. Investigators believe she is one of the guests that stayed in the hotel.

West Baden Springs Hotel
West Baden: 8538 W. Baden Ave.

This hotel (now hotel and casino) was host to wild parties, especially in the roaring 1920s. The times were good and the wine, women, and money were in ample supply. When the stock market crashed, at least two men jumped from the building to their deaths, signaling the end of decadence.

For many years, the fate of this hotel was uncertain. However, through investments and donations, this architectural wonder has been restored and is now reopen for business. And so are its host of ghosts.

Rumors of residual hauntings of the 1920 suicide jumps have been reported. Temperature drops occur on the grounds and within the building. Mists and orbs, as well as pale green lights, were reported on the second and third floors. With the renovations, these occurrences are still reported with more vigor. A man in a dark bowler hat in early 1900s clothing is seen walking along the third floor corridor. A woman in an elaborate gown is seen in the Atrium at night. Investigators who have spent several nights in the hotel have also reported EVPs of several people including a man who says "I've lost everything" and a woman crying. When asked why she's crying, the woman says "he's gone, it's gone". A brusque man is heard in the Atrium saying "It's too hot here." Staff members have reported seeing shadow figures and translucent figures in the basement of the building and at night. When the resort has slowed down somewhat, the sound of footsteps can be heard in the halls outside many doors. Guests hear mysterious knocks on their doors; when they open them to see who is there, they find themselves alone. Cold breezes play about the building. Staff and guests have also been pushed and slapped by unseen hands.

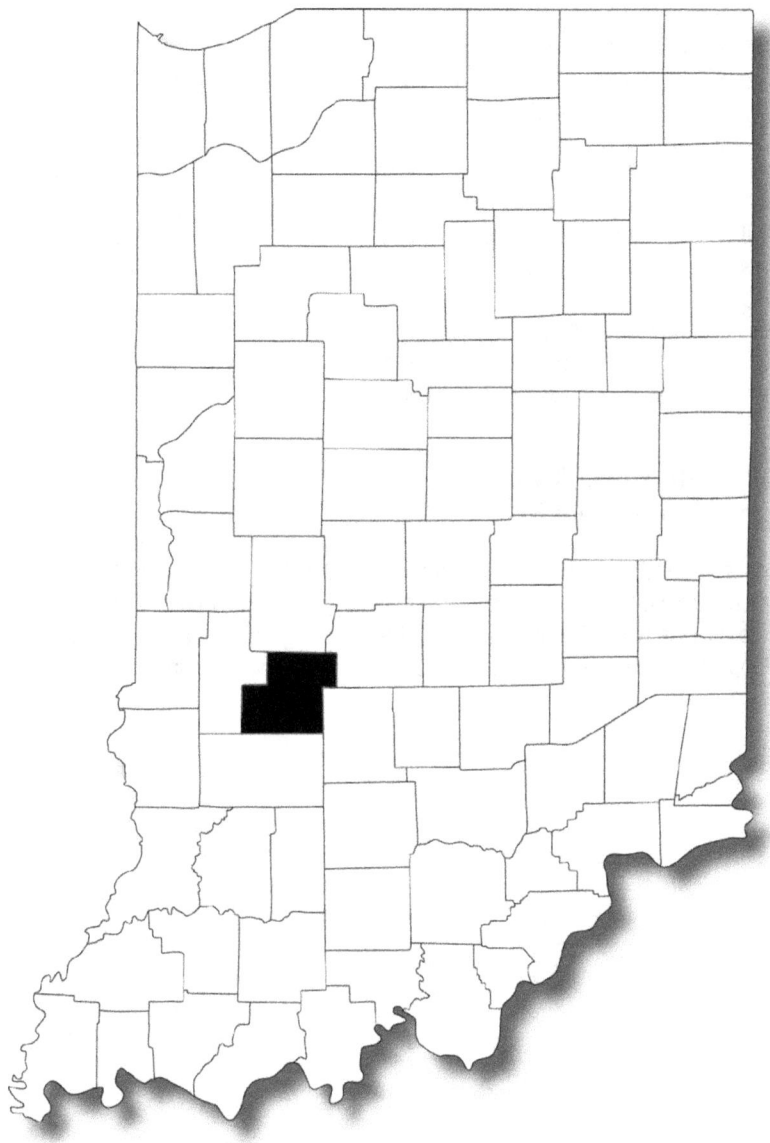

OWEN
COUNTY

Cagles Mill Lake

Cunot: Richard Lieber State Park is right next to it.

(Cagles Mill Lake is bounded on the east by SR243 and on the south and west by SR42.)
(aka Cataract Bridge; aka Cataract Falls Bridge)

Spanning the largest waterfall in Indiana, the upper falls have a sheer drop of 20 feet while the lower falls drop 18 feet. On Halloween 1878, robbers killed a man on his way to Cloverdale. Today, this man is seen on the bridge walking towards his destination. A Civil War soldier was also killed by highwaymen on the bridge. He appears to visitors as a bright light, culminating into a solid or translucent vision.

SR 42 used to run through this manmade lake. A man who lost his fortune in the stock market during the Depression hung himself from the bridge. On dark quiet evenings, walks on the bridge, the rope around his neck. He jumps off the bridge and sometimes he walks alone on the road and watches cars pass by him.

McCormick's Creek State Park Hotel

Spencer: 451 McCormick Creek Park Rd.

Reports claim this building was an insane asylum, which is untrue. From 1888-1914, it was a sanitarium, which treated chronic diseases, including mental health issues. Most times sanitariums were used for people who had the means to pay for the services; otherwise patients would find themselves at home coping with disease or in the case of mental health, in a state hospital. People hear screams, crying and footsteps when no one is around.

PERRY COUNTY

Fox Ridge Cemetery
Kitterman Corner/Siberia: Off Chaplin Rd, west of SR145 and north of I64

John Davidson was hanged for kidnapping a girl, although he proclaimed his innocence. Two weeks after he was hanged, the girl reappeared-married. The men who hung Davidson were never convicted. The cemetery is home to Davidson's body, with a fieldstone that has a noose on it and the statement "Vengeance is mine, saith the Lord." Investigators at the cemetery have heard an angry voice speaking. Asked if it is Davidson an affirmative answer is given. Asked what can be done to help him the voice states, "Liars".

River Road
Cannelton/Tell City: River Road (CR 334) can be accessed through the Ohio Scenic Byway near Cannelton or via Boundary St. in Tell City.
(aka Brazee's ghost)

A horseman with a whip was seen in 1858 by the Brazee/Schuster wedding party. Thirty-two years later, a boy was riding the same stretch of road and saw a horseman brandishing a riding crop. Today, reports of a phantom horse and rider are still reported, most noticably by the sound of hooves, the snorts of the horse, and the sound of the whip. The figure has been seen in the moonlight as a pitch black apparition.

Tell City Library
Tell City: 2328 Tell St.

The intercom buzzes when no one is waiting. Books appear out of thin air, and fly from the shelves. Mysterious figures seen throughout the library. Footsteps are heard on second floor.

Virginia Place
Cannelton: 205 Taylor St.

Moving orbs are recorded. The ground floor living room is the most active room. An apparition was caught behind an investigator in photo. Child ghosts playfully move items. Faces of children, men and women have been caught in multiple pictures- children, men and women. It is believed that the ghosts are that of Isabella de la Hunt, her husband, Civil War Officer Thomas de la Hunt, and their children, who lived in the home during the late 1800s until the early 1900s. Reports of square orb sightings have also occurred. Legend has it that Thomas killed the son of a black maid, because either he was the father of the boy, or he was jealous of the man who was. EVPs indicate that Isabella was not abused, but that her husband did commit the deed, have also been recorded. Furniture is sometimes shaken in the home. Other spirits include a little girl, a little boy, a black dog, a pretty woman and a mean-looking man.

PIKE
COUNTY

Austin Arnold Road

Winslow: Austin Arnold Rd.

An old man destroyed his own property when coal mines contemplated moving out toward his land. Later, he shot his dog and eventually himself. Some versions of the story state the man killed his family as well. One building remains on the property. Cold spots and feelings of unease and heaviness are felt at this location.

Blackfoot Cemetery

Spurgeon: 2.5 miles NW of Spurgeon on CR900S, southeast of Meridian Rd.

The cemetery dates from mid 1800s. Strange lights have appeared- blue, green and red. Much ado centers on a gravestone that is completely separate from the others in the middle of the cemetery (although this could be due to the age of the cemetery). A witch is allegedly buried in the cemetery and local folks believe this is her grave

Gullick House

Petersburg: 9th Street and Main Streets (razed)

The Gullick house was built by a local merchant, Jackson M. Kinman. Richard, the son of Jackson, was killed during the Civil War. His mother wouldn't allow him to be buried and instead put him in the attic. Eventually, she relented and her son was buried. The Case family rented the home from Kinman. The two Case girls, Hattie and Sarah, used the attic as a playroom until they saw Richard's shadowy figure in the corner. He watched but never spoke to them. Eventually, Sarah married and moved out, leaving Hattie and her husband Mr. Gullick in the home. When the house was razed in 1941, Hattie told several people about the ghost and wondered what had become of him.

Some local people believe he is still around. He is seen at various locations on the corner where the house stood, looking sad. Two investigators tried to speak with him when they saw him, but he disappeared immediately. No EVPs or photos have been captured..

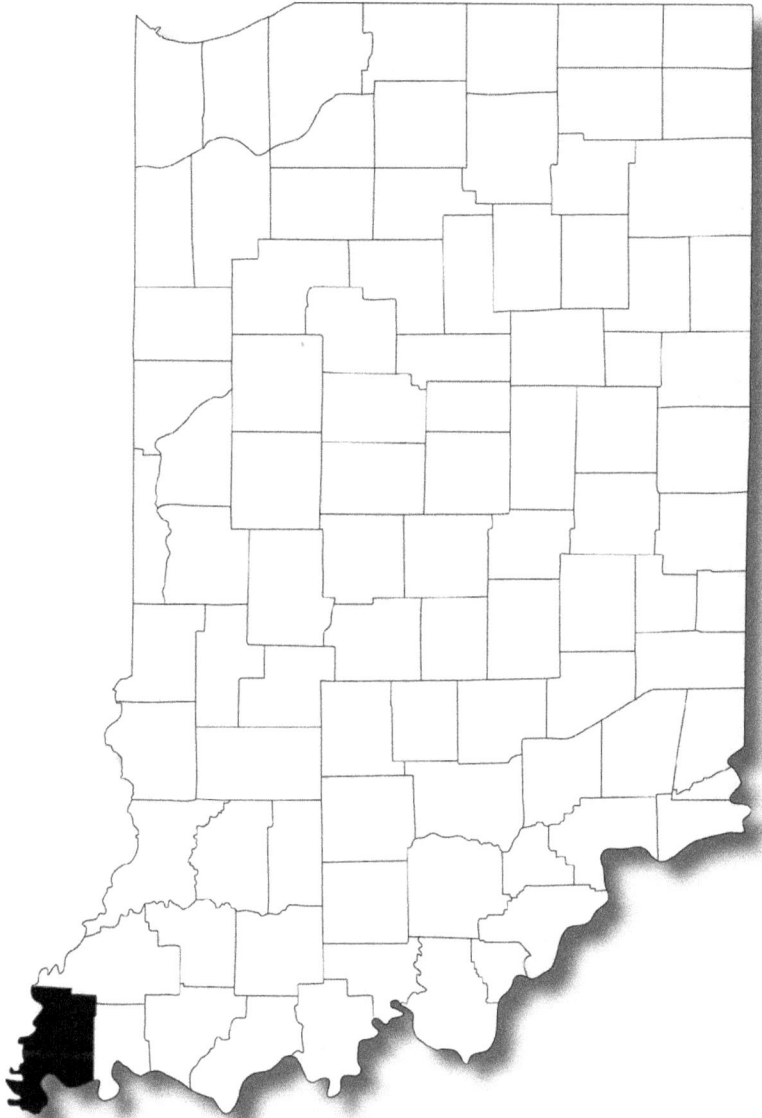

POSEY COUNTY

Griffin (town)
Griffin: Griffin off of I64 and SR69

The town was almost destroyed during the Tri-State tornado on March 18, 1925. It killed 58 people and injured 202. In the days after the tornado, you could only reach the town by boat. Only part of the schoolhouse was left. A year later, the school, the church, the grain elevator, and most of the homes were rebuilt.

In town, various people- men, women and children- are seen walking. Sometimes screams and moans are heard. There has been some speculation that Sydney Hyatt is one of the spirits. He was found under piles of bricks between the only restaurant in town and the general store. Other possible ghosts could be that of Clarissa and Vera young, sisters aged 14 and 9 respectively who were killed during the tornado.

New Harmony (town)
New Harmony: On SR66 next to the Illinois/Indiana boarder.

As the home to two historic attempts at communal living, New Harmony has a rich history. From 1814-1825 the Harmonists under Johann George Rapp and from 1825-1928 under John Owen, worked and prayed together in a utopian-like setting.

The town in general is the site of many paranormal events. Groups of shadow figures are seen in the local cemetery. Translucent groups of people walk from the south side of North St to the north side. The Working Men's Institute is home to several odd occurrences, including a man in blue who is seen walking with a book in his hand.

EVPs recorded include chanting and speaking in German. The EVP is believed to have said, "We must pray now" and loud laughter from a male voice. Lights throughout the town mysteriously turn on and off. It is not uncommon to feel cold breezes pass you even when it is very warm outside.

Poseyville Library
Poseyville: 55 S. Cale St.

The first library was established in Poseyville around 1825. The second was part of the town hall in 1901. The third came from a Carnegie endowment in 1905. In 2000 the library was renovated and expanded. As part of that process, the Hansbrough Inn (built ca. 1890) was demolished. The library staff and patrons believe now that they are haunted by the ghosts that moved in from the Inn.

The library owned the old Hansbrough Inn, which closed in 1910. The library had apartments in the building. The basement of the old inn was a dining room for train passengers. Cleaning staff, who normally lock themselves in the building, hear the opening and closing of the main entrance doors, although no one was found in the building. The consensus is that the library's ghost is a female and wants to be a caretaker of the library. The ghost has been seen in the basement of the library as the mist of an older woman from a different time. Other staff members have seen her as a grey mist in the basement, and on the northeastern corner.

One reason for the haunting could be that room was recreated using an historical picture. Computer issues and lighting problems abound. Installed programs uninstall, lights burn out in an unusually short amount of time. Disks go blank and DVDs become unplayable, despite having been played previously. Usually it is the computer room that has lighting issues first, then the Carnegie section, on to the Lamar room and then the hallway.

Robin Hill
Mount Vernon: 917 Mill Street
(aka Popcorn Hill, Ferndale, and Belden Place)

Built in 1837 (or 1838 by some accounts), one legend states the original owner, William Lowery, helped slaves on the Underground Railroad. When his daughter fell in love with and became pregnant by a former slave,, he killed the man and his daughter in her room. The room is supposed to contain blood stains and a residual haunting of this event. Every time people paint over the spots they reappear. Supposedly the daughter collected porcelain dolls and the dolls are still in her room.

Lights passes through the upper window. A baby giggles in the basement and people whisper throughout the house. Toilets flush and general noises are heard at night.

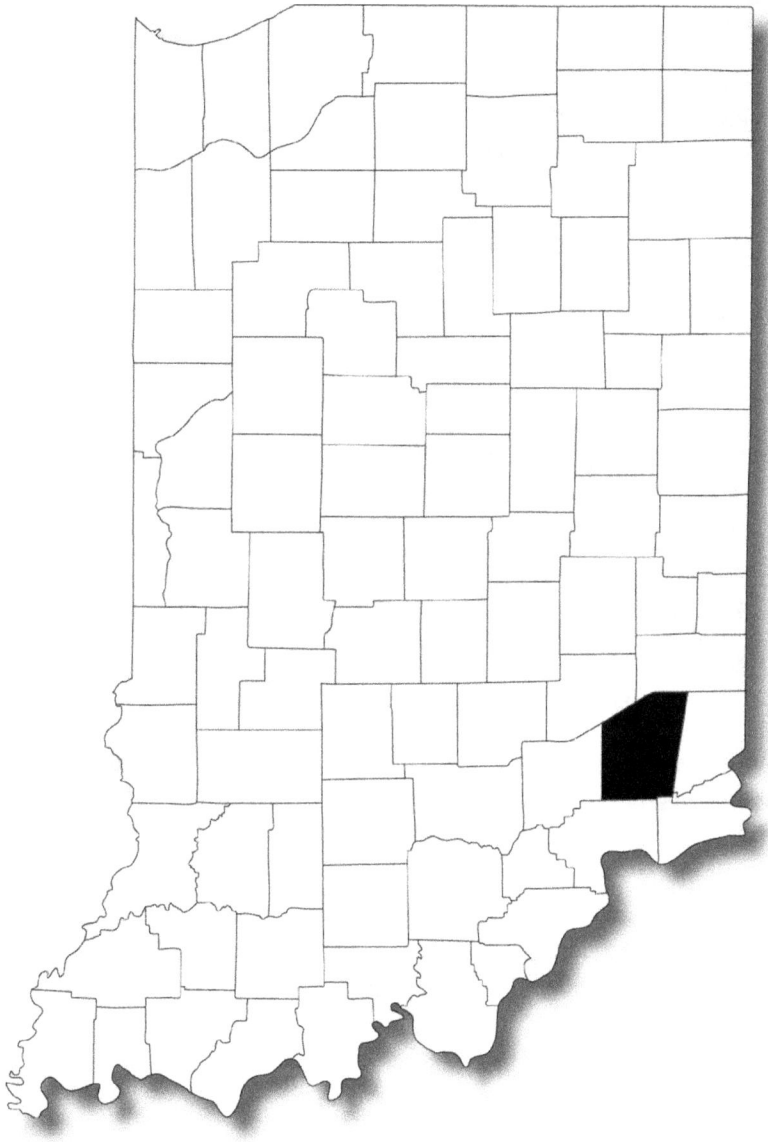

RIPLEY
COUNTY

Bonaparte's Retreat
Napoleon: 8961 N US 421

This building has been a variety of businesses, including a tavern and inn and was once a stop on the Underground Railroad. A female apparition appears to guests in the eatery and on the stairway. Her perfume can be smelled in the basement where fugitives were hidden during the Underground Railroad years.

Devil's Elbow
Osgood: N. Delaware Rd. and N. Milan Versailles Rd. SW of SR129

This local road is inhabited by evil spirits. A man was killed many years ago on the road, but the hauntings have predated his murder. Some people believe it is the evil spirits that provoked the murder.

Glowing red eyes, a milk-white figure of a woman, and a baby crying have been reported. This area affects your car; it will either stop working, or the headlights will dim without assistance.

Central House
Napoleon: On the square (Main Street)
(aka Newman House; aka Hicks House)

Built in 1838, this historic building has been used as an inn, a doctors office, several saloons, apartments, restaurants, and a stage coach stop. Several paranormal events occur which are tied to a girl named Jessica, who died from chicken pox, in 1865 at the age of 13.

She plays in the child's room and laughs. During tours, the rocking chair rocks, books move from shelves, and cold breezes whirl around the stairs. The clock in the house also has a habit of striking outside of normal times in abnormal ways.

Jessica also likes it when people play music in the house, especially the organ. She hums and sings to the music. The organ also plays when no one is using it. The lights in the house move and sway for no reason. Investigators report seeing orbs, doors closing and doll heads moving.

St. Louis Cemetery
Batesville: East of S. Mulberry St. at the end of Schultz St.
(Note: Batesville is in Franklin and Ripley Counties)

The cemetery is part of St. Louis Catholic Church. Burials began about 1869 in the cemetery. An Indian woman is said to haunt the cemetery. She was chased by the townspeople and buried alive. Her tomb is supposed to have a stone door as a top marker with a fence of iron bars around it.

Silver Bell Nursing Home
Versailles: 6996 S. US421

This 29 bed patient facility was a hotel before it was a nursing home. Lights go off and on in empty rooms; the staff hear children playing and people whistling when residents are asleep. The presence of invisible people is felt throughout the building. A nurse's aide was locked in a laundry room by an unseen presence and had to climb out a window.

Sunman- Guildford Park Bridge
See Dearborn Co.

Versailles State Park
Versailles: Off of US50 near Versailles

A soldier named Silas Shimmerhorn deserted the Confederate army and became one with the wolves around Versailles. He feasted on farm animals and shared his lot with the wolf pack. Eventually, the farmers got wise and found his hideout in the Bat Cave (now in Versailles State Park). Silas and the wolves were not there. Now people report seeing the pack of wolves at night, sometimes accompanied by a man. They hear the yelps of the pack as they approach.

SCOTT
COUNTY

Austin High School
Austin: 401 S. US31

A Spanish teacher who died in a car accident roams the school. Teachers, staff and students have seen her walking the halls, mostly at night. She was supposedly very fond of the Beatles and as the story goes, if you play their music, she will come. Custodial staff have quit after door handles to rooms they clean start rattling, and the area turns freezing cold.

Old Railroad
Blocher: Between N. Blocher Railroad and N. Blocker Main Sts.

A woman was killed on the track and a ghost train replays her death. As you watch, you'll see the woman appear. Her foot seems to lodge in the track. As she tries to free it, the train runs through her and you hear her scream.

Bridge Water Cemetery
Scottsburg: East end of E. Bridgewater Rd. near Kinderhook Lake

Legend states that Civil War soldiers were buried in the cemetery. African-Americans were not allowed to be buried there. Some African-Americans were hung in the cemetery. At night, handprints appear on your car and shadow figures move mysteriously through the tombstones. Temperature fluctuations are felt and several people report having been followed by a transparent white horse.

Investigators and visitors experience temperature drops and see glowing eyes in the trees. EVPs of spirits telling people to leave are frequently recorded. Other visitors speak of a demonic presence with glowing red or yellow eyes. Many investigators have had their electrical equipment and cars die without warning. Others have seen a night watchman in the cemetery. The transparent man is supposedly buried in the cemetery and his headstone glows as people enter the cemetery.

Haunted Slave House
Scottsburg: Liberty Knob Rd. (CR500S)

An old house rumored to have housed slaves sits back in the woods. Visitors have reported feeling sick and feeling malevolent feelings in the house. Some visitors claim to have been scratched and poked hard enough to leave marks. At least three people claim to have gone through a time warp in which they have seen African-Americans chained and lined up in the house "like cattle".

Liberty Knob Rd. and Bloomington Trail
Scottsburg: CR500S and S. Bloomington Trail. Taylor Rd. Between Liberty Knob Rd. (CR500S) and S. Bloomington Trail.

A misty fog appears bringing with it Confederate Civil War soldiers. The sound of metal on metal and the scent of gunpowder, leather, and sweat are also sensed. Some visitors hear fighting with the sounds of guns firing, swords clanging and the sounds of men screaming in agony.

Not everything is war-related. One man who lived nearby was in his barn working and felt he was being watched. Looking up, he saw a soldier, who has since reappeared many times. Once, while riding late at night, the same soldier guided the man back to his home, telling him to be careful, as he was about to hit a tree branch.

One person reports having her car stall on that stretch of road. She was aware of the legend and as she was walking back to town, she felt very uneasy when she heard a horse behind her. Turning, she saw a transparent Civil War soldier on horseback. He asked her if she needed help. Stunned, the woman stuttered, "Yes" and she was instantly lifted onto the horse. As the horse trotted off, she reports, "I don't remember the trip back to town. All I remember is being dropped off at the outskirts of town." She was able to stop at a friend's home and solve her car issues, but it will be something she never forgets.

Scott County Home

Scottsburg: 1050 S. Main St.
(aka Scott County Heritage Center and Museum)

This former county poor farm was originally built in 1879. In 1892 this building was replaced by the brick one that exists today. Many a family who had lost all money and hope moved into the farm. To stay on the farm, they were expected to work. Today, the building is the Scott County Heritage Center and Museum. Many of the people from the original farm are still seen walking around the property

Babies cry, lights turn on and off, and strange smells permeate the area. Footsteps sound on the upper floor when no one is in the area. Bells ring without anyone pressing them and no one is there. The front door opens and footsteps entering are heard. Employees hear their names called and feel a woman's presence. A mental patient named Mary lived there her whole life so they named the ghost after her.

SPENCER COUNTY

Eureka Road

Rockport: Eureka Rd. (later W. CR50S) is off of S. 9th St. in Rockport. Note: No train tracks currently exist on this road, which runs to the IN-KY border.

Reports of different residents hearing men having a conversation and a spectral train when there is none on the tracks. They have also heard a man calling their name and the televisions turn themselves on and off. Children have also complained about toys moving across the floor, and of seeing horses running through the upstairs.

Mathias Sharp House

Rockport: 319 S. 2nd St.

House is a home for Katherine Sharp who went from farmer's daughter to well off matron. Both husbands, Mathias Sharp and Mr. Batchelor, (whom she married after Sharp) became ill from supposed food poisoning and died. Although she was acquitted of both deaths, the Sharp children continued to believe she killed her husbands.

The documented haunting go back to at least 1916 when it was documented that on wedding nights, breaking glass was heard by the occupants. Some people have witnessed the event. Additionally, Katherine's black clad figure is seen walking around the house inside and out muttering about how she was "robbed" of her home.

Rockport Inn

Rockport: 130 S 3rd St.

This bed and breakfast is over 100 years old. One owner's wife died there. She can now be seen in the rooms, and heard walking and humming.

Sunset Hill Cemetery

Rockport: SW of old SR 45, bordered by S CR25 W and WCR100 S

Visitors see a demonic presence wearing a dark cloak.

SULLIVAN
COUNTY

Antioch Cemetery
Cass: East of N CR800E on E CR100N (at junction of N CR875E)

On foggy nights around 1:30 am, a man dressed in a dark colored suit with flowers in his hands can be seen looking down at a grave. Witnesses also see shadows of people flashing past and over their vehicles, accompanied by scratching and tappings heard.

Bethel Cemetery
Hymera: On SR48 east of S. Church St.

The Nathan Hinkle grave and monument (Revolutionary War soldier/casualty) glows. If you call his name, he will talk with you or manifest in the form of a mist.

Free Springs Bridge
Ferree: CR 175 W across the railroad tracks at the bottom of the hill.

Many murders took place over the years at this bridge. A headless man roams around looking for his head. A phantom hobo that was ran over by a train is also seen. A couple had a car accident in which she was killed. The man was never found. He is heard calling her name throughout the area around the bridge.

SWITZERLAND COUNTY

Schenck Mansion
Vevay: 206 West Turnpike St.
(aka Shank Bed and Breakfast)

This home has two legends with the truth somewhere in between. A woman named Sarah lived in a cabin and took in Civil War soldiers. When she took in Confederates, the militia came in, tied Sarah and a soldier up and burnt the cabin. After their deaths, no one seemed to know the Confederate soldier's name- until it appeared written in the dirt. Once the ghost was named Ed, the writing in the dirt stopped.

When the current Victorian home was built, it stood empty for a long time. It didn't help that the ghost would bother the African-American workmen in the home. When the family moved in, the son of the owner felt someone touch him and pinch his "bum". Male visitors to the home have seen a solid apparition of a young woman and report kisses bestowed upon them. One woman witnessed the apparition as well.

Another variation of this story is that a husband and wife lived in this home until the husband was sent off to war. During the war, his wife cheated on him. When he returned home, he found his wife and her lover in bed. He killed them and himself. They replay that fateful day many times throughout the year in the evening. Additionally, the woman touches men who enter the house. The husband yells to get the men to leave.

VANDERBURGH COUNTY

112 Franklin Street
Evansville: 112 Franklin St. *(razed)*

This incredibly active location had a portal in the living room. It has now been razed because no one would stay in the house for long.

123 Michigan Street
Evansville: 123 Michigan St.

An older woman is seen in the windows when no one is home.

24 Monroe Street
Evansville: 24 Monroe St.

The basement of this home had a painting of woman knocking on door holding a lantern with flowers in it. The painting covered the whole wall next to the stairs.

Investigators saw an entity in basement, and painting on the basement wall. Suddenly, something under the stairs grabbed onr person's legs leaving red marks. The attic had a pentagram drawn in charcoal on the wooden floor. The area seemed charged with negative energy.

205 Florida Street
Evansville: 205 Florida St. *(razed)*

The home has rooms under the attic eaves. On the stairs to get to the rooms, a dark entity pushes people down. A child saw a man in black who was not nice and laughed very evilly. Once, when one of the occupants was left alone, she had a feeling she needed to leave but stood her ground to finish vacuuming. She told the negative force she would be done soon and to leave her alone.

In an upstiars room, many people reported hearing "get out" by unseen people. A residual haunting of a man getting a haircut was seen in the upper story kitchen. The home also had a woman who would cry in the upstairs bathroom. Psychics said that that someone had committed suicide. Footsteps are heard on the porch. The person who rented the upper apartment for many years felt that the majority of the spirits were protective because the people in the apartment below were drug dealers. On another occassion, a man kneeled next to a Native American who was visiting the occupant. He told her the man was a spirit guide who was just checking in with him. One child who lived in the apartment watched a bird come in the window and said it talked to her, telling her things that only her family would know.

The child's mother believes it was her grandmother, who always wanted to come back as a bird. Another male occupant heard his name called and heard his uncle call his name as well- his uncle was not in the house. Another occupant who was crying saw the presence of a woman behind her as a reflection in the mirror- the entity had her arms around her and wanted to know why she was crying.

A humorous incident involves dishes flying out of the cabinet. The apartment occupant told the spirits, "If you want me out, get me a winning lottery ticket!"

One eerie incident involved a woman waking up and seeing her husband standing by the windows. She called to him, sat up and saw not her husband, but a demon with red eyes and a crisp pointed robe (not like the KKK). She stared, blinked, and it was her husband again.

578 Baker Street
Evansville: 578 Baker St. *(razed)*

This apartment had a furry black shadow figure in its back apartment. Upstairs, there was one room that was not part of any apartment. The curtains in this room would move all the time. Many times men were heard fighting on the stairs, occupants would open the door to find out what was going on and no one would be there. One ghost figure of an old lady used to walk up the same stairs with a ghost cat in her hands.

649 East Maryland Street
Evansville: 649 E. Maryland St.

Late at night cards could be heard shuffling in the kitchen, as if someone were playing a game. There was also a transparent woman seen in the kitchen at the sink looking out the window. The house also had an extraordinary infestation of odd, abnormally large, spiders of many species. Two other women ghosts walked through the living room area while staring at a renter. They then moved into the next room and disappeared through the wall, which was once a door leading outside.

814 E. Franklin Street
Evansville: 814 E. Franklin St.

The Victorian house was built at the turn of the century, and later used as apartments. A male entity walks the main hall downstairs in the early evening and late at night. It sounds as if he is pacing and waiting, and he seems to be wearing older style heavy soled boots. Pots and pans would clang and bang when no one was in the kitchen downstairs. This continued nightly after the tenants vacated, leaving the upstairs renters all alone with the spirits, boot steps, and noisy cutlery. A woman in white is seen in the upstairs in several rooms, and a cold, strong breeze was felt by the upstairs renters teen daughter when she was home alone. No one stayed in the apartments for long because of the activity.

1929 Stringtown Road
Evansville: 1929 Stringtown Road

Parents died here and now haunt the location looking for their children.

7831 Seminary Road
Evansville: 7831 Seminary Road *(razed)*

The old farm house that used to sit on this glorious hill is now gone. Inside lurked several people. An older man was seen sitting in a chair just as transparent as he was. An older woman used to look out the front window. The front door would open of its own accord, even though it was locked. Athough it is not certain, investigators believe these ghosts were former owners who have just chosen to stay in the area.

8513 Rainier Drive
Evansville: 8513 Rainier Dr.

Owners see the ghost of a tall man in a black suit with bowler/jazz hat who carries a suitcase. Many times he walks into the bathroom and disappears. The children have also seen the "suitcase man" walking through the home, going up or down the long hallway. Additionally, a black shadow haunts one of the rooms. It casts a bad feeling about the home.

The area around this home is generally haunted. The woods next to the mobile home park are haunted by shadow people and a dead local farmer, which adds to the atmosphere. A trailer sits near the property on which a girl was raped and brutally beaten by her mother's boyfriend.

Angel Mounds
Evansville: 8215 Pollack Ave.

Native American sun worshipers lived at this location for hundreds of years. It is unknown why they left or were wiped out, no indication of a great war has been found. Unusual graves have been discovered. Visitors have seen residual hauntings of people who lived there in former times. A procession of people carrying a small body has been seen. Crying and laughter have been heard on the grounds, as well as chanting and mysterious drumming.

Big Ditney Hill
Evansville: Big Ditney Hill is surrounded by Weyerbacker Rd, Greenbrier Rd, Wasson/ Lilly Pad Rd. and Seven Hills Rd. Two roads come off Lilly Pad Road that lead to access of the hill.

The Irishmen who built the Wabash and Erie Canal got very ill and many died. A mass grave was dug. The ill who would probably die were thrown in with the dead. One intrepid man clawed his way out one evening, and it's said he killed the foreman for allowing such a thing to happen. The foreman is said to roam the hill on moonlight nights and is known as the Ditney Man.

Boehne Camp Hospital

Evansville: Boehne Camp Rd. *Privately owned and torn down in 2007. The buildings across from the old hospital are being renovated into apartments.*
(aka Evansville TB Hospital)

Ghost patients roam this old TB hospital grounds. The ceiling of the old hospital was known to drip blood. A rocking chair in the building would rock by itself. One explorer found himself without the use of a thumb after a visit. Patients are still seen although the hospital has been razed. Sometimes visitors have heard tortured screams as if someone was in pain.

Carpenter House

Evansville: 405 Carpenter St.

This home was built by Willard Carpenter in 1849. Staff and visitors hear strange noises and see items levitate.

Dogtown (town)

Cypress: Dogtown Tavern: 6201 Old Henderson Rd

Dogtown has the reputation for being a very haunted area. The river bottoms are full of stories about the dead rising from the waters. Stories of mob and gangster burials along the banks of Dogtown are also told. In the dark woods around Dogtown are many unknown gravesites left to be reclaimed by nature.

Three most notable haunted places are:

Haunted School House: A man raped and killed two girls in the basement. You can hear the girls screaming at night. Additionally, the abandoned homesites on the way to this location are full of shadow people and orbs.
Dogtown Tavern: The doors open and close on their own and the lights flicker. A couple of transparent men sit at the bar from time to time. (Note: Tavern is now closed)
School: Drive along Old Henderson Rd. until you get to a gravel road. Follow this road until you're about to go into the woods. The house is privately owned and under renovation.

Eastland Mall

Evansville: 800 N. Green River Rd.

A security guard was killed at the mall. You can still see his transparent figure walking around checking the stores.

East Mary Street

Evansville: East Mary St.

A Lakota man had been adopted by a white man and his Hispanic wife. He grew up in this house. He sometimes stayed there since his mother needed help and had become disabled due to the disease lupus. "Ron" was sitting in his old room very late one night listening to the radio when the music changed to a show about the death of JFK. Ron's mother really liked JFK and there were several pictures of him around the house, in Ron's room. Ron looked at the picture of JFK in his room and it was glowing. Ron heard the picture say, "I am not gone."

Evansville Christian Life Center
Evansville: 509 S Kentucky Ave.

Formerly the Monastery of St. Clare, it is now home to a not-for-profit organization dedicated to the "restoration of people".

Legend has it that on June 8, 1985 construction workers came in to removal. The DNR came in to remove burials from the monastery. As they finished up their work, a bad storm came through. Ten years later at the same time, another bad storm came through (1995). Every 10 years on the anniversary date of the removal, a bad storm is said to come through. People believe the nuns are unhappy that their burial place was disturbed.

Today, people say they hear footsteps walking behind them and they feel entities watching them. Staff and residents have also seen the shadow figures of nuns walking from room to room throughout the building.

Evansville County Courthouse
Evansville: Fourth and Vine Streets

On January 18, 1973 Anne Kline was stabbed 19 times in a basement alcove of the courthouse. She was a math teacher at Lock Year Business College and was conducting courses down in the courthouse basement because the college had suffered a fire. The crime is still officially unsolved.

Visitors to the old courthouse have felt a "desperate" presence in the building, especially in the area of the murder. Several investigators have had to leave the area because of the negative energy. People have reported feeling ill as well. One investigator saw a pool of blood on the floor and tried to take a picture of it. When he saw the picture, it didn't contain blood, but it did contain a white mist that had not been visible at the time the picture was taken.

In the catacombs, Investigators report electromagnetic field disturbances. On one investigation a bottle of clippings of news stories about murders and missing people was found. A spirit has been seen floating in the same room. When approached, it runs by the witnesses, leaving them with a feeling of dread. Temperature spikes and cold spots are also felt.

Evansville State Hospital
Evansville: 3400 Lincoln Ave.
(aka Southern Indiana Hospital for the Insane; aka Woodmere)

This mental hospital was commissioned in the 1880s and established in the early 1890s. It followed the same destructive path as the other state institutions- overcrowding from day one, a lack of knowledge about the budding mental health field, and therefore untrained staff. Later it also suffered from lack of trained employees even after more became clear about the field of mental health. In 1943 several older buildings were destroyed by fire, but the newer buildings remained. In mid-2006 the remainder of the old buildings were razed with only a small section of modern buildings left.

When the burned buildings were still partially erect, staff and patients would see lights go on in the buildings, when there was no electrical hookup. Shadow figures would walk the campus, the burned buildings and even in the newer 1940s buildings. One patient saw the distinct figure of a person going from room to room, turning on lights and bending down as if they were checking patients. He said it went on from one floor to another until he could no longer see the person on the opposite side of the building.

In the 1940s infirmary, trays rattled when no one was around. On Ward 8 (B8) on the third floor, something that sounded like a bowling ball rolling across the floor above it was heard- it would hit the wall and start over again. The odd thing is that there was nothing but roof on that floor.

In the same building, in 1989, in the corner room, phantom footsteps were heard walking through the building. Staff and patients alike reported seeing shadow people walking behind them and beside them. Staff and patients also felt a presence, as if something was not quite right in the building.

In the G/H building (newer building with fence) a patient felt like something evil was watching him in the mirror, as if it didn't want the man there. He later found out a different patient committed suicide in the room. In G ward basement, a white ball of light bounced through the rec room and went through the windows and outside. The staff and patients watched it move across the lakes and go towards St. Mary's. It went across Lincoln Ave over the buildings there and disappeared.

Several suicides occured in the buildings and several patients jumped from windows. Some of these patients could be seen as ghosts reenacting their demise years after their deaths and their screams could be heard.

Now that the buildings are gone, some of these patients can still be seen as mists, orbs, and apparitions on the grounds. EVPs of screams and insistent cries for help have been captured.

Hangwell Tree and surrounding area

Evansville: Hangwell tree and old man sighting: Godeke Rd. (CR 550 N) Corner of Schultz Rd.

A strange coldness and cloying dread falls over this area. Recently someone has built a house by the old maple tree. Legend has it the tree cannot be cut down. Old timers know of this tree and the legends, but no one can provide history or why the area is so haunted.

Visitors see people hanging from tree. A male ghost walks the road in front of the tree. The Beast of Hangwell roams the fields around it. Full body apparitions appear in and around the tree. Shooting stars are seen gathering at the tree. As one group approached the tree around 2:00 am, one June, a full-blooded Lakota Indian saw the surrounding trees turn into lion's heads and he would not approach the tree. Other visitors approached the tree and saw a red-headed woman hanging from the tree in a long, pink, sheer gown. Under the tree leaves, dark shadows of "a 100 other people" hung with the woman. These people held books, and wore trousers, shoes.

Another visitor on the expedition remembers playing ball with a little boy in knickers , and who had a little dog with him. Some of the visitors came a few hours later at daybreak and went by a house (see below) where a man was leaning against a stop sign. They told him they were going to visit the tree and he nodded- disappearing before their eyes. On the way to the tree, viewed across several acres of plowed fields, was a glowing gold skull on the tree trunk. Upon close examination, there was no patterning on the trunk to give this illusion.

During another visit, shadows played over the ground, blocking the exit from the area. As the group tried to move away from the tree, the shadows followed them. Finally one member of the group distracted the shadows and the rest headed to the road. Eventually the other member was able to run and escape the enclosing shadows.

Henry Reis School
Evansville: 1900 Stringtown Road

A shop teacher died and now haunts the school. Tools turn on and off. Hand tools disappear. Students report ghostly footsteps and cool breezes.

Home near the Ohio River
Evansville: SE First and Monroe Streets *(razed)*

Occupants saw a bleeding Revolutionary War soldier in basement room under the front living area. The home is no longer there but the agonized cries of a man are still heard.

Howell Wetlands
Evansville: 1101 S. Barker Ave.

Investigators have seen a woman in a pale pink frilly dress by the banks near the bridge

No 6 School
Evansville: SE corner of No. 6 School House Rd. and Big Cynthia Rd.

The apparition of a man is seen in the windows.

Little Ditney Hill and Gander Cemetery
(aka Little Ditney Cemetery; aka Lockyear Cemetery)

Evansville: Booneville-New Harmony Rd. and Gander Rd. Go north on dirt road. Gander Cemetery is on Little Ditney Hill

Note: Some visitors mistake Gander Cemetery for Young or Youngs Cemetery (which is on the Boonville- New Harmony Rd.)

The Gander and Lockyear family cemetery sits on Little Ditney Hill. The interments date from 1899, although because of spotty records, these could go farther back. A pterodactyl-like creature roams the area. So does a band of Native Americans. The Indians are reported as dark shadows with white outlines. An unidentified man in black walks through the trees.

Pidgeon Creek

Evansville: Located at Diamond Ave. and Pidgeon Creek. Park at Garvin Park and walk on grass near levy. If you go down Heidelbeck and go next to levy, you'll have to drive into gravel. Go from First Ave. to Heidelbach Canoe launch, along Pigeon Creek Heidelback Ave to Negly Ave to Baker Ave to road that goes to creek.
(Note: Now the creek has overflowed, and is overgrown with random types of trees.)

In Garvin Park a demon lies in the ravine. Visitors hear screams. A group of visitors investigated one night and one asked the demon to present itself. Shooting stars appeared and a sinister fog rolled in, circling the group. A "flat paper man" with a bowtie smiled and danced sideways between the levy and creek with his arms moving. He split into two people- one white with black bowtie, black with white bowtie—both danced towards each other. One investigator got a severe headache and saw native people dancing around the tree.

Two big rock-shaped moving tannish-brown mounds with sharp razor teeth were coming for them. Moving along the creek, behind tree, coming up the dirt road. One investigator warned another. Grass started moving without wind. As the investigator got on the road, creatures start moving slowly. A little tree next to them (now has a copper fish hanging from it), started swaying like dancing. One investigator saw something in the old cotton wood tree- a grey fog mass sparkling on edges. It rises up, gets past the top of the tree, turned into a moon shape with soft edges, bursts, and twinkly stuff falls into tree to the ground. They decided to leave, as fog was very close to them, and one investigator was pregnant.

Pollack and Lodge Streets
Evansville: Pollack and Lodge Sts.

This property was once one of the area's most prolific farms, boasting many barns and a very large grand house with two wings. The family spent many wonderful years there till tragedy seemed to strike all of them all at once. The gentleman took his older son with him into the Dubois County area to sell some cattle and buy a couple of horses. The man and his son conducted business and stayed at an inn, where they were both killed in their sleep for their cash and the two grand horses they had purchased. No one was ever convicted of their murders. The father and son lay in state before burial at their home on Pollack Ave. It was a hard winter and the widow had seven more children to care for with no husband and no older son. It was cold and the widow shut all of them into one room on the second floor to keep warm. A lamp tipped in the night, or a chimney fire started, burning part of the house, and the family suffocated to death.

Another the burned portion was rebuilt, the house was sold. The house kept changing hands frequently, even after it was turned into apartments. Renters wouldn't stay. Every two or three years, the former burned section would catch fire, and then it would be rebuilt. Owners and renters would see a shadow man in the backyard smoking a pipe. You could smell the cherry tobacco. Frequently children could be heard laughing and playing, small pranks would occur to the living. On

Christmas every year the smell of popcorn would permeate the space of the house. Apple pie could be smelled as well. Late into the evening sounds of laughter and many guests partying would be heard. Glasses clinking, laughter of adults, murmured conversations, and carols being sung could be easily heard as well.

In the last ten years the rest of the land and barns were sold off for a subdivision, and the old house is still there as a four-plex apartment building.

Residual haunting near Hangwell Tree
Evansville: S. Newmaster Lake Rd. Stop sign on curve.
(See Hangwell Tree entry. Past Hangwell Tree around the next curve.)

The man burned to death in house. It's said the man killed wife in home. He was abusive and she fought back. He raped her with a stick of firewood. These acts are a residual reenactment.

Reynolds House
Evansville: 611 Harriet St
(Now a medical clinic in downtown Evansville-Doctor's plaza)

A ghost of a 19-year-old named Oscar haunts this house. He died in 1922 and has been seen and heard ever since. He runs up the stairs and shuts windows during storms. One 12 year old girl saw him on the stairway and later in the room where he died. He is said to have followed the Reynolds when they moved to their new home, yet he has still been seen in the area by people visiting downtown.

Salems Kirche
Evansville: South Welborn Rd.

Former renters report phantom church bells ringing at five in the morning, but upon going outside, the bells become silent. The abandoned church also has a misty ghostly woman who sits in the front of the church as if still in prayer. The antique piano in the church will play mysteriously at dusk and dawn. There are graves of several pets beside the church, but the stones are usually overgrown by weeds. One of those pets was a much loved canine of the former renters. He is seen as a misty wolf like form at the edge of the woods. A shadow man is seen exiting the church from the back door and sometimes the wider side door. He is usually hunched over as if he is dragging something heavy.

There is a clearing to the north of the church where an old barn and forge stood. You can sometimes hear the whinny of horses and the stamp of their hooves during the day. Shadow figures of men and women are sometimes seen in the surrounding woods which abound with deer.

Another ramshackle barn is at the end of the long driveway. Strange footprints have been found in and around the barn, similar to those of a large bird or reptile. The pond down the hill from this barn is home to a little boy spirit. During the Depression era he drowned there trying to rescue his pony. The pony had become entangled in some barbed wire near the pond and couldn't get loose. The pony drowned there too. Sometimes late in the evening you can hear both of them thrashing about in the water.Sometimes hear the boy's cries for help can be heard.

South Sweetser Avenue 1700 Block
Evansville: S. Sweetser Ave. 1700 block *(razed)*

Former renters report a crawl space hatch in the floor of the kitchen. It would never stay shut. Growling could be heard late at night when a person was brave enough to venture into the kitchen for a glass of water. One fateful night the utilities quit working, then would come on and off at random intervals. The renter's dog and hamsters were going crazy with a nervous frenzy. The floor hatch started to bang up and down, cold spots and breezes were felt in the house. The occupants went outside to await a brother-in-law who was coming to work on a car. As the brother-in-law arrived, a horrible, evil groaning could be heard coming from the house to the front yard. Whatever it was tried to coalesce as a grey mass floating ten feet above the ground, then it landed with a very loud band on the hood of the non working car.

There was also a boarded up upstairs formerly accessible by a wooden staircase outside the house. It too was boarded over. A local man had been dealing drugs and child porn from the apartment upstairs. One night someone came, argued, and shot him. His blood stain remained on the floor upstairs, and on the downstairs ceiling. His footsteps had been heard upstairs as well as a weekly reenactment of the shouting and shooting.

A year or so later investigators went to the house. The landlord did not show up with the keys, but the neighbors said the house had caught fire each time it was rented in the previous year. The last time caused the utility company to completely disconnect the house from all wiring. The back was open, and there was a foul decomposition odor coming from the kitchen. The house was in very bad condition and the blood stain was still on the ceiling. Bumps and bangs were heard upstairs, and a tenant recorded an EVP saying "No, no, don't."

Tekoppel Elementary School
Evansville: 111 N. Tekoppel Ave

Three young girls at day camp went to the girls bathroom and got an odd vibe from the storage room located there. Several people have reported bad vibrations from spirits that are said to haunt the building. The maintenance area holds spirits of children and a mean adult man. The lower level is the most haunted. Investigators captured lots of orbs.

University of Evansville- Paint Studio
Evansville: USI has a great campus map on its website.

Items move in the studio. At night, soft misty figures are seen in the studio and hallway. At present, it is not known who the entities are.

Willard Library
Evansville: 21 First Ave.

Willard Carpenter opened the library in 1885. He was a successful businessman with a daughter, Louise. Legend states when Carpenter died, his daughter was so bitter that the fortune was left to the library and not her, she is trapped there as a spirit.

Women's Restroom (basement): When the library was still on coal heat, a man who came in every morning to shovel coal for the day saw the grey lady watching him- he left and never came back. In the women's restroom. Conversations from bodiless people are heard here, doors open and shut without occupants, and the water turns on and off.

Childrens' section: Books have flown off shelves, aimed at adults and children. Some of the stuffed animals have moved their heads and talked to children and investigators. Additionally, one child and her mother saw the dollhouse lights come on- although it has none! Visitors feel cold spots and the rocking chair rocks on its own. Sometimes the mist of the grey lady appears. Visitors have also reported smelling the scent of lilacs.

Main area: Louisa is believed to be the grey lady seen in the library and on its webcam both in the main area and children's area.

West Side Sportsman Club
Evansville: 1000 N Peerless Rd.

Ghostly children play by the lake. No one knows if these were children who came to the club, or if they were children who died on the property at an earlier time.

VIGO
COUNTY

1100 Seventh Avenue

Terre Haute: 1100 Seventh Ave.

A man nicknamed Uncle Seddy, George Sedwick Mankin is seen in this home. He was a coalminer who died in this home, August 10, 1928. He is buried at Highland Lawn Cemetery. His figure has been seen gliding from room to room and sitting in the living room. Temperature drops occur when he makes his appearances.

2425 6th Avenue

Terre Haute: 2425 6th Ave.

Once an orphanage annex for African-American children, many strange occurrences have happened in the home including seeing small children. The ghost of a 9 year old boy haunts the house. He is very mischievous and hides items. He is also very curious and likes to rummage through drawers and boxes.

Fontanet

Du Pont Powder Company *(aka Fontanet Brick Plant)* : 2 miles north of Fontanet. It is an unmarked woods.

Fontanet: North of E Rio Grande Ave on N Baldwin St.

(aka Fountain, Fountain Station, Hunter)

On October 15, 1907 sparks fell on some loose powder and the Du Pont Powder Company exploded at 9:15am. The first explosion came from the glazing mill. Three other explosions followed. At 9:45am, a second explosion came from the press room and another one in a smaller mill building. At 10:45am the heat from the fire caused the thousands of barrels of powder at the powder magazine to explode.

Seventy to eighty people were employed at the mill. When the second explosion at the powder magazine occured, it injured physicians who were trying to triage the injured. People who died in the explosion didn't all die immediately. Dr. Carroll, who was burned to a crisp begged to "be shot". Superintendent Monahan was blown to bits and burned. His wife was burned to death in the home they lived in at the mills. Two half sisters escaped.

In Fontanet all the buildings were smashed to the ground, although no one was hurt in the town. A brick schoolhouse a quarter mile from the scene was damaged and many children were hurt. Windows as far away as Brazil and Terre Haute shattered. In all over 40 people died and 250 were injured. People in Cincinnati felt seismic **waves** from the blasts.

Interestingly, Fontanet was a mining town that was operated by the Coal Bluff Mining Company. Coal Bluff was two miles north east of Fontanet.

Alfred I. duPont had remarried that unfortunate day and interruped his honeymoon to survey the damage. He vowed to rebuild it all, and so he did, with the exception of the mill itself. The people left in the town begged him not to because they were scared.

The place where this plant was now looks unnatural. It is a wooded, private piece of property. A large amount of dead trees litter the place. The area is haunted. If you visit the location on the day of the accident, you can see the glow of the furnace and fires, hear the explosion and hear the screams of the dead and dying. Visitors also report feeling intense heat, smelling burning flesh, and being touched by hot hands.

Fontanet has a bean dinner every year to commemorate the explosive event.

Fruitridge Avenue and Hulman Street

Terre Haute: Fruitridge Ave. between Hulman St. and Margaret Ave.

Young men and fast cars are nothing new in any town. Fruitridge Ave in Terre Haute has seen its share of late night competitions. One has become legend. As two cars challenged each other one hot summer night, and a nameless young man blew a tire near Hulman Street. His car spun out of control and crashed into a huge brick wall. The boy was thrown through his windshield and smashed face first into a wall. For many years now, some say you can still see the face of the youth staring out of the rock where his life ended.

Highland Lawn Cemetery

Terre Haute: 4520 Wabash Ave.

A dog, Stiffy Green, and his dead owner, John Heinl, walk the cemetery at night. The dog was in the mausoleum of the owner but the cemetery staff removed it because of people roaming the cemetery after dark. Heinl died in 1920 and soon after, despite care of local residents, the distraught dog died as well. He was added to the mausoleum to be with his owner.

Honey Creek Mall

Terre Haute: 3401 S. US41

A very pale man in an old-fashioned suit, carrying flowers is seen in many shops, sometimes by multiple people at the same time. He doesn't interact with anyone. Some people believe he is a ghost from a different time. Other people believe he is an incarnation of Death. He is also seen exiting the mall quickly. Usually it seems he is following someone who recently exited as well. When curious visitors follow him, the figure simply disappears.

Indian Orchard

Terre Haute: Oakcliff Rd. and Wabash River

The Delaware Indians occupied this area from the early 1700s. A girl living among the Native Americans, Lena, had been taken from white parents in Pennsylvania when she was a child. A time came when white captives were to be returned. Lena was asked to leave, although she'd been raised by a chief. The person who was to take her away, Nemo fell in love with Lena. When she was reunited with her brothers and sisters (her parents had passed) she couldn't forget Nemo. Eventually the two snuck away and took vows before the Great Spirit.

When they returned to the tribe at Terre Haute, they found that her village had been destroyed in a tribal fight. As they settled in the area, one evening warriors from the Miami tribe tried to kill Lena and her son. Nemo fought to save his family, but succumbed to the enemy arrows. Lena threw her son to the Delaware men and killed herself with their knife. The Miami raised her son in honor of her bravery.

This battle can be seen reenacted along the banks of the Wabash.

Indiana State University
Terre Haute: Indiana State University has a great map on its website.

Blumberg Hall: Students report items missing and moved. A woman who threw her child down a trash chute haunts the building. The Resident Advisor gave birth in the residence hall but got rid of the baby because she didn't want to lose her place at school and on campus.

Malloy's Pub
Terre Haute: N .7th and Lafayette Streets

Visitors see orbs and moving objects. Investigators report batteries dying while on location. Visitors also feel as if they run into something solid, like another person even when nothing is standing in front of them. Owners and customers have also detected a spirit of a railroad worker, and a child named Sarah, who likes to play tricks on customers.

Old Mill Dam
Markles: Off Rosedale Rd. and Mill Dam Rd.

This was part of the Underground Railroad. A small transparent girl stands by or in the creek.

Pi Kappa Alpha House
Terre Haute: US 40 and Scott Ln.
(aka Glenn Orphan's Home)

In 1987, the Pi Kappa Alphas had no clue what awaited them in the former orphanage. The fraternity makes its home on part of a 26 acre wooded property, with more than a half-dozen buildings. Members of the fraternity see the front door of old dormitories open and close, yet no one appears.

The main building of the fraternity was built in 1896, and the majority of the other buildings followed soon after. Although some buildings have been destroyed and others added over the years, it is now a property full of the best and brightest people at Rose-Hulman.

Opening doors aren't the only tales. Visitors hear children splashing in water and laughing when no such child is around.

Something knocks on the front door and when answered, no one is there. This phenomenon has happened quite a bit. One young man took to his room when he heard the knock at the door and found no one. As he closed the door, he heard the knock again, except it came from a room under the staircase.

Some of the orphanage buildings do not belong to the fraternity, but they are haunted, nonetheless. Children have been seen playing outside the property, bounding in and out of trees. Their laughter for some students is sometimes deafening.

Preston House
Terre Haute: SE side of 13 1/2th and Poplar Streets' Fowler Park 10654 Bono Rd *(razed)* *(aka Dewees Mansion)*

Originally from France, Major George Dewees was a harsh man by nature. When his son was scalped and killed, he began to guard his house with hungry dogs. Depending on which story you hear, Dewees was either a Underground Railroad operator or rumored to have a thriving slave trading business. Regardless of the outcome, Major Dewees threw himself into his work. When his marriage failed and his wife, Matilda, wanted to leave, she became mysteriously "out of town" for an extended period. Eventually people began to suspect foul play and upon inspection, it was believed that the Major interred his wife in the walls of the house. Dewees was never investigated, but the house was never more unlucky. It was rumored after his death that the home was part of the Underground Railroad, but no evidence of that has been found. Several times the home was targeted by fire bugs. Eventually, it was left to crumble. When the home was eventually razed, the workers were told to look for the body. It was never found. Parts of the razed home including stone and woodwork, are now part of the gristmill in the Pioneer Village at Fowler Park.

Legend has it during Dewees time and for many years after, his wife's spirit was seen coming from the fireplace into the room or she was seen sitting on the chimney, sometimes accompanied by a blue light. Still today, the now-empty lot is home to a woman believed to be Matilda. She appears as a white apparition, sometimes crying and is surrounded by a blue light. Although no connection with the underground railroad was historically made, investigators have captured EVPs of spiritual songs while investigating the lot.

Interestingly enough, the Fowler Park gristmill has its share of paranormal activity. People claim to feel a very angry presence in the mill during different times of the day. Additionally, the angry voice of a man has sent people running when he tells them to leave. Finally, several visitors report running into an invisible form as they've walked around the structure. Could this be the Major, unhappy that his home was torn down or used for other purposes?

St Mary of the Woods College
St Mary of the Woods: Located on Hwy 150 just outside of Terre Haute in St. Mary of the Woods, Indiana.

- Theatre: This is home to an apparition best described as a floating nun that on occasion can be seen late at night, as well as hearing footsteps of someone running up and down the stairs when there is no one else in the building.
- Tunnels: under the campus (sad to say they are closed to the public): Spirits have been seen and heard.
- O'Shaughnessy Hall: Blood stain that looks like is a face in a wall. The stain came from the early days of the school in the 1800's when a nun took her life. Many attempts to remove the stain have been made. When it appears

to have been cleaned it mysteriously re appears days later to the same form and color which it was before. Note: This hall is no longer there. A new dining hall with the same name is in its place.

- Foley Hall: A nun who was an art teacher didn't get to finish a painting before her death. The face of her subject wasn't finished. She is said to haunt the hall without a face. Late at night, in the cold 2nd floor art studio, other girls see her but can't see her face. Sometimes it is clear that you can't see her, other times she stands in shadow. Footsteps and noises as if a skirt is rustling have been heard. Torn down in 1987 but she is said to migrate.
- Guerin Hall: This is probably the most active building on campus. Particularly rooms 333, 334, 346. An invisible nun tucks students in at night. Her measured step precedes her touch.
- LeFer Hall: Lights turn on and off. Shadowy nuns in old habits are seen flittering around the dorm.
- Grotto: The Virgin Mary puts in appearances during the Fall
- SMWC Cemetery: Shadow figures abound throughout this cemetery. At times, they are interactive or shift into different colored mists. One investigator reports seeing a shadow figure shift into a light pink figure which then morphed into a wispy mist that came toward her. As she backed out of the cemetery, it followed her until she reached the grotto.

Shadow Beasts

Terre Haute: Off US40 on 675W. Turn left at the end of the stree, you'll see shadow beasts run with the car on this road.

Shadow figures and a beast run next to your car. When you try to shine lights on the beast, it disappears. Yet when you shut your light off, the shadow figures and beast return, moving with your car.

Terre Haute Country Club Golf Course

Terre Haute: 57 Allendale

Apparitions and orbs appear nightly. At the 6th hole, a child named Alex walks. As the legend goes, Alex got drunk, passed out and died. He vomits and screams for help.

Terre Haute Regional Hospital

Terre Haute: 3901 S. 7th St.

Nurses see deceased patients. Room 540 has a cancer patient who is seen (west end of 5th floor). Nurses tried to track her down as a wandering patient, but when they went to find her, she had disappeared.

Vigo Co. Historical Museum

Terre Haute: 1411 S. 6th St.

Orbs and mists are captured in pictures. The orbs tend to stay around the main staircase. At one time a private home, this building has been home to a halfway house, and is now a historical museum.

The old crib in one of the upstairs exhibits moves occasionally, even though the area is closed off.

WARRICK COUNTY

Heilman Road
Chandler: Heilman Rd.

There is a dessicated cemetery that sits on a hill top off the gravel road. EVPs captured include moans and wails as if someone were dying. A black shadow chased investigators out of the area one evening. When they returned the next day to retreive equipment, they found recordings on their cameras consistent with the wailing and moaning heard by others. Unseen hands are moving the video camera through the area until a dark figure appears with glowing white eyes. It comes toward the camera and the camera drops to the ground, leaving the watcher with screaming.

Mt. Carmel Register
Mt. Carmel: 115 E. Fourth St.
(aka Dailey Republican Register)

An old ghost named Caesar haunts the building. Papers go missing and visitors hear footsteps and voices when no one is around.

Scales Lake
Boonville: Off of S. Parklane Dr.

Black Annie is believed to haunt this lake. Black Annie (or Annis or Agnes) is a witch/crone-like woman who delights in killing people, children in general. This is a Celtic legend which has crossed to our side of the pond.

Silent Room
Boonville: Unknown
(note: This location is sometimes attributed to Tennyson, Indiana, but it is in Boonville)

The story goes that 5 women were killed in a shed off this road by the land owner. People feel watched and an overwhelming feeling of dispair surrounds the place. Supposedly the shack was soundproofed for the murders and you are unable to scream inside the shed. Additonally, some people feel that they've been pushed and clawed at inside the building.

Warrick Publishing/Boonville Standard
Boonville: 204 W. Locust St.

People feel strange vibes and feel as if someone is running past them. Investigators hear tapping noises in the basement. An EVP captured asked the spirits what their favorite color was answered with the word "green". Investigators also felt touches on their arms and backs and saw shadow figures move through the building. Investigators and staff also caught orbs on film. Investigation equipment malfunctioned on site, leading some investigators to believe spirit activity was afoot.

Yankeetown Bridge

Yankeetown: Yankeetown Rd. bridge over Little Pigeon Creek

A woman hung herself from the bridge. Investigators have been able to hear her jumping and the crack of her neck and the swinging of her body from the bridge.

WASHINGTON COUNTY

Bradie Shrum residence
Salem: E. Hackberry St. (You can't miss this one- it is a three story brick, Gothic, Italianate home)

Home is supposed to be made up of bricks from the second Salem courthouse. An elementary school teacher is said to haunt the building, going about her daily business but never interacting with people.

Crown Hill Cemetery
Salem: The closest road is St. Michaels Rd. SE.

A stone of Caddy Naugle is of a little girl by one of the gates. Her stone was carved by an unknown stone mason. She had gotten sick and died. Caddy haunts the cemetery in search of the mysterious man who showed her daddy kindness in carving the stone.

Not to be confused with the Crown Hill Cemetery in Indianapolis (see entry), this cemetery is located in a wooded area bounded by Buck Creek. No standard roads lead to it.

(East) Washington School (Middle School)
Pekin: 1100 N. Eastern School Rd.

This school has several areas that are said to be haunted, although the school has no explanation for them. In the third floor girls bathroom, lights switch on and off at will. Many students have seen the switch move by unseen hands. Additionally, the toilets flush on their own and the stall doors open, close, and lock without anyone being in the restroom. In the old gym on the basketball hoop, a handprint that looks like blood is said to appear and disappear. Some students believe the handprint appears before sports games as a sign of bad luck. Custodial staff has also witnessed the events, and have heard footsteps echoing the hallways when no one else is in the building. Cold spots precipitate these footsteps.

French House
Pekin: 8178 S SR 335

Items move around from one spot to another. A little boy about eight, with dark hair, overalls, and no shoes roams the home.

Goose Creek
Salem: South of SR 56, close to Mill Creek Rd.

A woman spends her time throwing rocks in the creek. When you approach her, she'll
give you an annoyed look and disappear. A man with severe head wounds walks through this area as well. He doesn't interact with you.

Henderson Park

Salem: Henderson Park Rd. into park. Take gravel road to creek.

Local lore states that in the 1970s, three girls were murdered by a cult in the cemetery. A man took the three girls to the cemetery on the promise of a party. Instead the girls were sacrificed, leaving their souls to haunt the Henderson Cemetery, which is said to be on park grounds.

According to local historians, no such cemetery by that name exists in the county. The Old Smedley Cemetery (Mount Pleasant-Old Smedley Cemetery) is on the grounds of Henderson Park.

In the park on the path near the creek, investigations and visits have turned up mists, voices and feelings of dread and discomfort, although nothing has been recorded as hard evidence.

Indian Spring

Indian Spring: S. Mill Creek Rd. between W. Fort Hill Rd. and W. Wilson Ln.

Although her identity is a mystery, a woman with a switchblade sticking out of her back is seen walking along the road. Some people speculate she is a settler, but others say she was an unsolved murder case from the mid-1900s.

Katie's Lane

Salem: E. Farabee Rd. at S. Eastern School Rd.

A drunk man tipped a tombstone on himself and died. The police have ruled it unsolved and were puzzled that he could tip over a one ton stone. Legend states that a house exists across from the Blue River Baptist Church and that before the house was built, strange lights were seen and odd noises were heard.

Old Blue River Cemetery

Salem: Bounded between SR135 and S. Blue River Church Rd. This cemetery has no main roads to it and is in a wooded area.

Civil war soldiers have been reported standing against trees in the cemetery with their guns next to them. When approached, they nod to you and continue smoking. The closer you get the more they fade away. When they do disappear, you can still smell tobacco smoke.

Rotary Springs Camp

Hitchcock: Between N. Cox Ferry Rd and N. Rush Creek Rd.

A female ghost spends her time stacking rocks. She's been captured as a mist on photos.

Salem (Town)
Salem: Gas stations of Salem

A dead delivery man is said to visit two of the gas stations in town. Although he pumps the gas, he has yet to pay. Apparently one gas station employee was ready to call the police when the car that was pulling away disappeared in front of his eyes.

Smith Miller Cemetery

Salem: Much debate concerns where the real 13 graves is. Many versions of this story exist all over the US and the UK. This one is Smith Miller Cemetery at the end of Baker Rd. on the banks of Blue River. To get to this cemetery go to the end of Baker Rd. You'll have to go through a field, into a gully and across a wooded area. It is private property, so you'll need permission to visit.
(aka 13 Graves)

Legend says that if you go through and count the graves one way, you'll count 13. When counting the other way, you'll only count 12. Once you've done this, one of the grave inhabitants is supposed to appear.

Index

G

H

I